Quebec

ANTHONY HOCKING

Publisher: John A. Savage

Managing Editor: Robin Brass

Manuscript Editor: Jocelyn Van Huyse

Production Supervisor: Rachel Mansfield

Design: Tibor Kovalik

Graphics: Pirjo Selistemagi

Cover: Brian F. Reynolds

THE CANADA SERIES

McGRAW-HILL RYERSON LIMITED

Toronto Montreal New York St. Louis San Francisco
Auckland Beirut Bogotá Düsseldorf Johannesburg
London Lucerne Madrid Mexico New Delhi Panama
Paris San Juan São Paulo Singapore Sydney Tokyo

QUEBEC

kilometres
0   25   50

© RAND McNALLY & CO.

ONTARIO (NORTHEASTERN SECTION)
QUEBEC (WESTERN SECTION)

kilometres
0   30   60

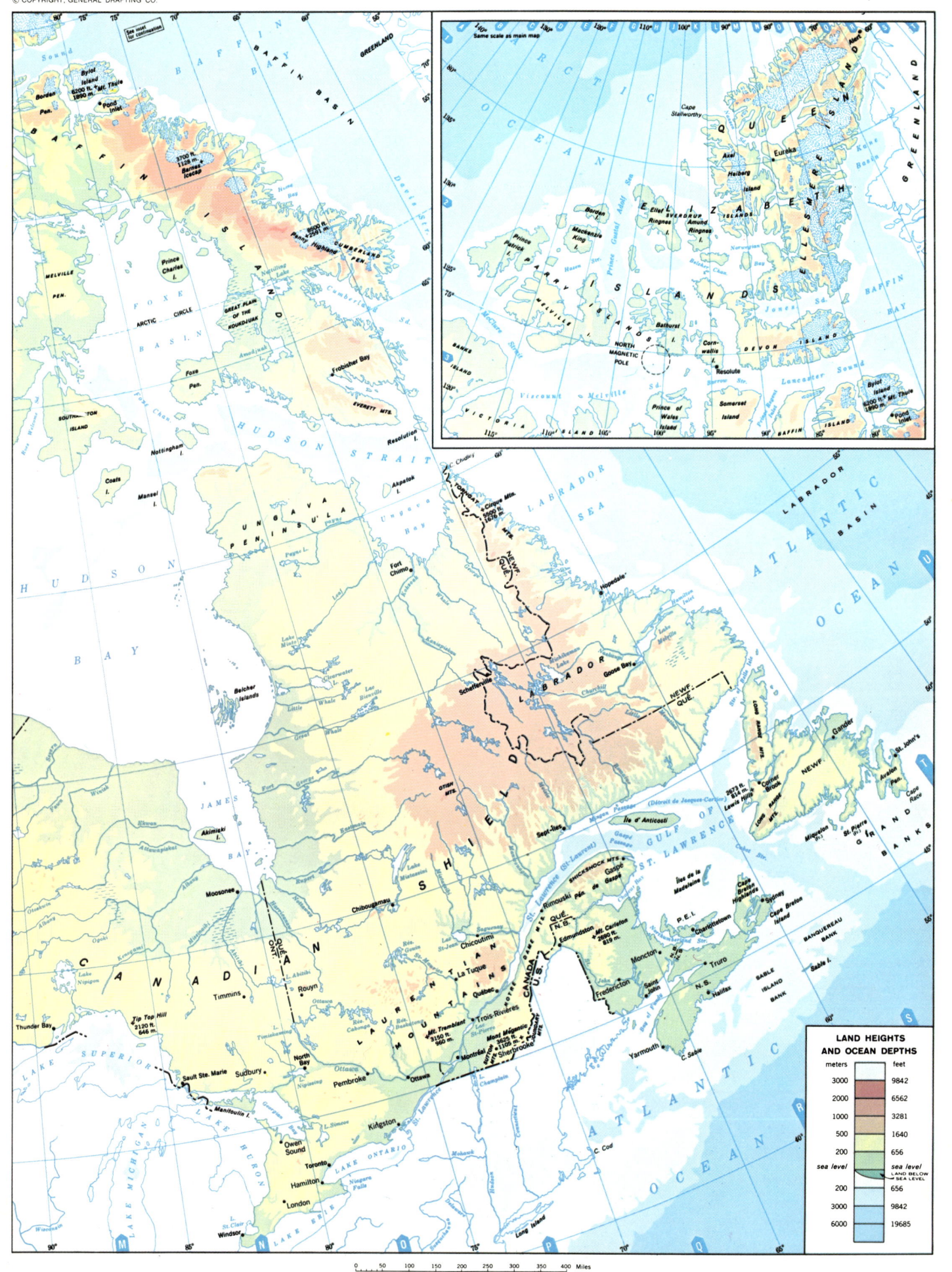

© COPYRIGHT, GENERAL DRAFTING CO.

LAND HEIGHTS AND OCEAN DEPTHS

meters		feet
3000		9842
2000		6562
1000		3281
500		1640
200		656
sea level		sea level / LAND BELOW SEA LEVEL
200		656
3000		9842
6000		19685

0 50 100 150 200 250 300 350 400 Miles
0 100 200 300 400 500 600 Kilometers

QUEBEC

Contents

Quebec is Canada's most historic province. It originated with Samuel de Champlain's *habitation*, built in 1608 on the banks of the St. Lawrence, and it has played a crucial part in the development of North America. Yet only now is its vast northern potential being developed.

The term 'Quebec' is Algonquian, meaning 'where the river narrows.' It was originally applied to the cape where Quebec City stands today. There Champlain established the first permanent settlement of New France. In the seventeenth and eighteenth centuries its young adventurers claimed half of North America for their king.

Following the English conquest of 1760 the colony's wide boundaries were slowly pinned back. In 1791 it became Lower Canada, and subsequently Canada East, and on Confederation, the Province of Quebec. Later, enormous tracts of Northern Canada were ceded to it — known today as New Quebec.

It is New Quebec that holds such great potential. Resources of the south have been developed nearly to their maximum, but the north holds immense reserves of minerals, hydro power, and forest potential as yet largely unexplored. Already vast iron ore deposits are being developed in the east, and the James Bay region is being opened.

Northern Quebec is more than twice the size of France, and Quebec as a whole is the second-biggest province or state in Canada or the United States. Slowly its hinterland is being settled. Quebec's one weakness is a lack of hydrocarbon fuels, but even without them the province could be Canada's richest within two decades.

Most of these possibilities are in the future, but Quebec has already experienced a wide-ranging cultural renaissance which has reasserted French Quebeckers' special place in North America. Society, the arts, and not least the French language have benefited. Modern Quebec is filled with echoes of past triumphs and promises of those to come.

Quebec's national flag was officially adopted in 1948. It signifies French authority (the blue ground), a Roman Catholic people (the white cross), and the heritage of New France (the four fleurs-de-lis).

THE SHIELD

Quebec, like Caesar's Gaul, is divided into three parts. At its heart are the sediments of the St. Lawrence valley, in the south and south-east are the Appalachian mountains, and in the north and west are the jumbled formations of the Precambrian Shield.

The term 'Precambrian' was coined when geology was young. Geologists dated rock strata by examining the fossils they contained, and the earliest they could find were in the mountains in Wales. The Romans had named Wales 'Cambria,' therefore rocks containing the early fossils were termed 'Cambrian.' Today they are believed to be about 400 million years old.

The early geologists recognized much earlier formations, which they could not date because they contained no fossils, and dismissed them as 'Precambrian.' No progress was made in untangling their secrets until William Logan's geological survey of the Canadas in the 1840s recognized a distinction between 'Archaean' and 'Proterozoic' rocks. Logan's Archaean rocks were very ancient, and his Proterozoic rocks represented a time of early life, for in them he recognized miniscule fossil traces. These classifications still stand.

Modern study of Precambrian rocks began in the 1890s, when an Austrian described what he called 'Shield' formations around the world. These formations are massive stretches of Precambrian bedrock following the contour of the earth's crust, and therefore are shaped rather like a medieval knight's shield. Nine such shields have been recognized, in Africa, the Americas, Australia, the Antarctic, Asia, and Northern Europe. Due to glacial action, Canada's is the most exposed.

Shields are the bases of continents and originated up to four billion years ago and more, though much has happened to them since then. In Canada, the Precambrian Shield is horseshoe-shaped and surrounds (and perhaps underlies) Hudson Bay. Its eastern half makes up 95 per cent of Quebec, and is known as the Laurentian Plateau.

During the present century geologists have made much progress towards understanding Canada's Shield, which is a rich hunting-ground for clues

▲
The Canadian Shield has been scraped and shaped by successive glaciers of the Ice Age. Glaciers bulldozed soil and vegetation from the north and deposited them on the St. Lawrence lowlands, where they provide the basis of the region's agriculture.

Thomas Patten's drawing of Montreal in 1760 provides a view of the 'royal mountain' — the westernmost of eight conical hills set in a crescent on the Montreal plain. They are the result of volcanic activity.
▼

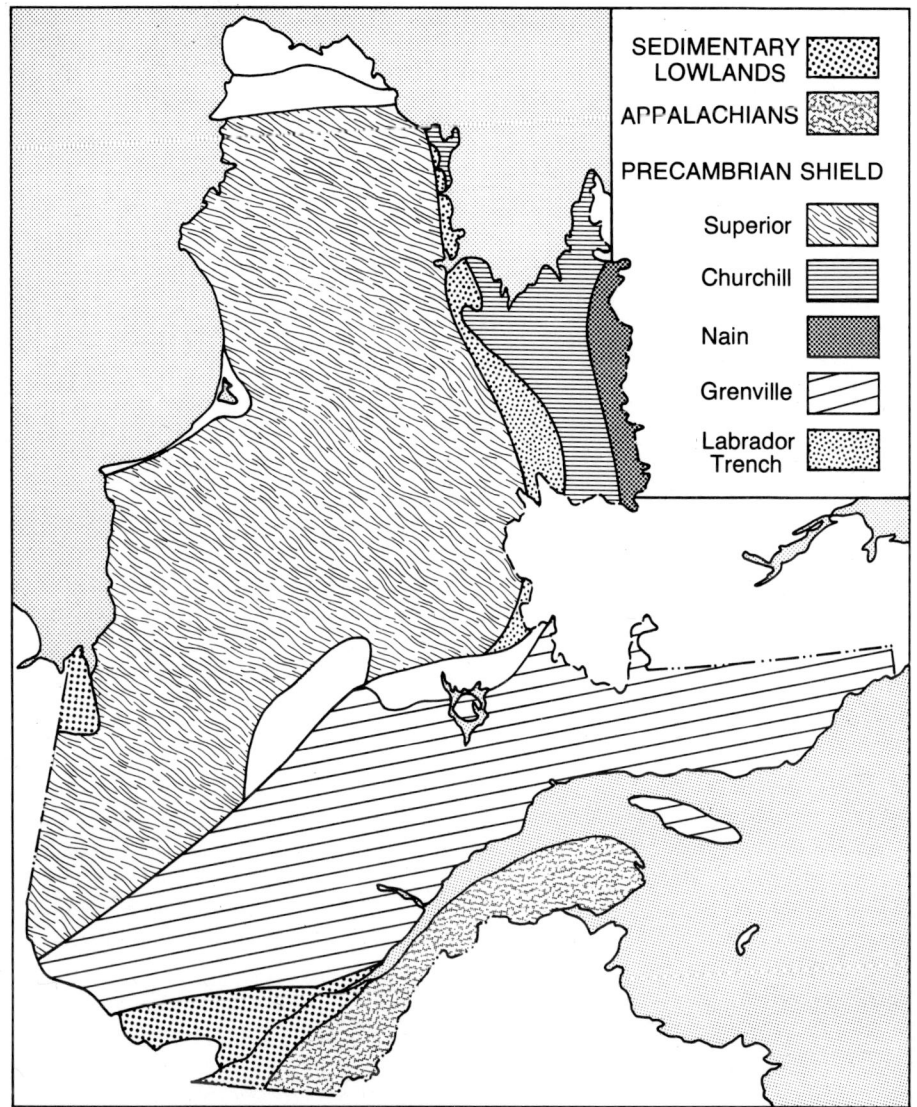

SEDIMENTARY LOWLANDS

APPALACHIANS

PRECAMBRIAN SHIELD

Superior

Churchill

Nain

Grenville

Labrador Trench

Geologists recognize three main geological zones in Quebec — the Precambrian Shield (with its various provinces), the St. Lawrence lowlands, and the Appalachians.

earth's crust collided, driven by energy released along an undersea volcanic ridge in the mid-Atlantic.

At least two main waves of mountain-building went into the Appalachians, which in Quebec comprise the Gaspé Peninsula in the south-east and the whole of the Eastern Townships in the south. The sediments themselves are paleozoic — formed between 200 and 600 million years ago — and are interlaced with lava flows and other volcanic rocks.

These volcanic interruptions introduced a number of important minerals, notably copper in the Gaspé. Base-metal deposits of the Shield, particularly copper in the west and iron ore along the Labrador trench, are probably of similar origin. The chrysotile asbestos found in the Eastern Townships is associated with ultramafic rocks originally under the ocean that were exposed and altered when thrust above sea level.

The third major geological region in Quebec is the St. Lawrence valley, which is composed of consolidated sedimentary deposits of sandstone, limestone, and shale. The region lies east of a promontory of the Shield (the Frontenac Axis) farther upstream. The sediments lie in horizontal beds that are frequently disturbed by faults and open folds.

to the origins of the earth's crust. A number of geological 'provinces' have been recognized. These provinces are the result of four periods of mountain-building or 'orogenies,' which metamorphosed the rocks.

The first of these orogenies was the Kenoran, dated at some 2500 million years ago. It left traces throughout Superior province, in effect all northwestern Quebec and extensive areas of Northern Ontario and Manitoba. The Hudsonian orogeny, of about 1700 million years ago, affected Churchill province up the Labrador trench.

The Elsonian, a localized orogeny of about 1400 million years ago, affected Eastern Labrador, a small part of Quebec known as Nain province, and

also part of Grenville. The Grenville orogeny, of some 950 million years ago, folded and metamorphosed rocks in Eastern Ontario and throughout Southern Quebec.

In time the immense pressures within the Earth that thrust up mountains have been outweighed by persistent erosion through millennia, particularly by wind, water, frost, and the sharp contrast between heat and cold. Such influences slowly decay rocks until the grains that compose them are washed away.

Much of the debris eroded from Grenville and other provinces went into the formation of the Appalachian mountains south of the St. Lawrence. Heavy loads of sediment were laid down. Later they were raised when plates of the

The village of Baie St. Paul on the north shore of the St. Lawrence is set on the St. Lawrence lowlands, but behind it loom the Laurentian mountains, the beginning of the Precambrian Shield.

LAND OF SNOW

On hearing of the English conquest of Quebec in 1760, the French author Voltaire suggested that the loss was not serious. He dismissed the little colony as 'a few arpents of snow,' worth considerably less than French possessions in the West Indies.

The view was typical of contemporary French indifference to Quebec. The little colony's 'habitants' were several generations removed from the great emigration boom of the seventeenth century, and French travellers in the eighteenth century brought home unflattering tales of the rigours of the northern winter — ice and snow from November to April.

What they failed to explain was that the habitants had long since learned to cope with the challenges of their environment. Winter temperatures plummeted far below freezing, but they were accompanied by dazzling blue skies and clear, dry air. There were storms and blizzards on occasion, but they were rare and lasted only a day or two.

To compensate for winter, summers could be hot — a point still missed by many visitors to Canada. Magically, a few warm days at the end of winter prompted an explosion of life in trees and plants which seemed to bypass spring, at least by European standards, and projected Quebec into the heart of the summer season.

In contrast the end of summer luxuriously extended itself into a leisurely fall, providing plenty of time to prepare for the winter ahead. Far from being a northern desert, as Voltaire evidently imagined, Quebec was *La Belle Province*, as later generations came to call it, and it was beautiful in all seasons, with or without snow.

The snow which Voltaire scorned was a considerable advantage in early Quebec, in that it made for easy transportation in winter in a country where no roads existed. The habitants adopted snowshoes from local Indians, introduced horse-drawn sleighs, and used horses to skid heavy logs from forest to watercourse to wait for the thaw.

Summer arrangements hinged on these waterways. The St. Lawrence river was Quebec's lifeline to the world outside, and early settlement hugged its banks. But there were other rivers, too, that were used as transport routes by Indian tribes, by the French explorers, by the *coureurs de bois* who opened the interior, and also by the logging companies of later years.

Tributaries joined the St. Lawrence from both the north and the south. Particularly important in early days were the Saguenay, flowing from Lac St. Jean and joining the St. Lawrence at Tadoussac, and the St. Maurice, which enters farther east at Trois Rivières (or Three Rivers) so named by early French who misinterpreted two islands in its estuary.

Montreal is sited at an even more impressive junction. From the northwest flows the Ottawa (which is itself

▲ In the maple and hardwood forest, fall is Quebec's most glorious season. This is a scene at Ste. Brigitte de Laval in Montmorency county, near Quebec City.

The Laurentian mountains provide magnificent scenery in both winter and summer, as at the ski resort of St. Sauveur des Monts in Terrebonne, north-west of Montreal. ▼

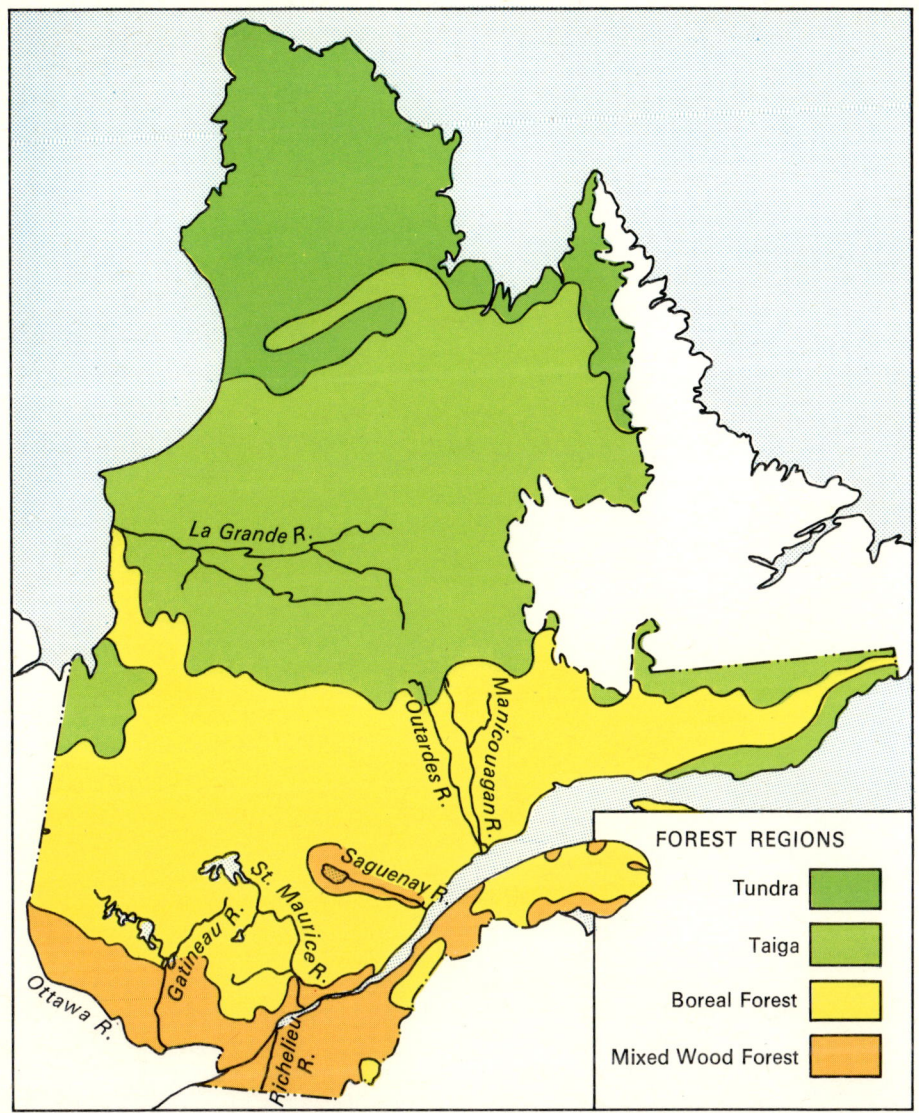

FOREST REGIONS

Tundra

Taiga

Boreal Forest

Mixed Wood Forest

Quebec is a land of rivers and forests. Zones of vegetation decline in abundance from relatively thick mixed forest in the south, through boreal forest in central Quebec and taiga in the north to barren tundra towards the Arctic.

fed by several tributaries); from the south flows the Richelieu, which springs from Lake Champlain and joins the St. Lawrence at Sorel. All these and the upper St. Lawrence, flowing down from Lake Ontario, were prime transport routes until the mid-nineteenth century.

The upper St. Lawrence remains important, following the development of the St. Lawrence Seaway. The Seaway has flooded most of the white-water rapids that punctuate its course upstream of Montreal, and conceals much of the river's interesting geology. It appears that the upper St. Lawrence is relatively young, for it has not yet cut its own bed. Instead, the river runs towards the sea by whatever route is easiest.

It is now the one means by which the Great Lakes of the interior are drained. Geologists believe that in earlier days the chief drainage channel was the Ottawa valley, and several ancient watercourses have been traced.

The twin rivers Outardes and Manicouagan enter the Gulf of St. Lawrence at Baie Comeau. All told the St. Lawrence system drains half the province. Northern rivers like the La Grande, now being developed as a source of hydraulic power, flow to James Bay or otherwise to Hudson Bay or to Ungava Bay on Hudson Strait.

Voltaire dismissed Quebec as 'a few arpents of snow,' but early habitants soon learned to cope with their new homeland's harsh winters.

Soil and Climate

The lower Ottawa valley and the area around Montreal see more than 140 frost-free days each year. Thus they have the longest growing season, which in Quebec is a more crucial factor to agriculture than precipitation and fertility. The southern shore of the St. Lawrence and a belt north of Montreal have between 120 and 140 such days.

Glaciers of the Ice Age dumped extensive glacial till on the St. Lawrence valley and in the Eastern Townships, providing valuable farmland. The commercial forest belt dominates the Shield to the latitude of James Bay, but gives way to barren sub-arctic taiga and eventually to bleak tundra in the north.

it was possibly a trading outpost of the Iroquoian-speaking Huron peoples, who lived farther west. Certainly some sort of fur trade was already in progress, perhaps encouraged by Basques from northern Spain and south-eastern France, who fished in the Gulf of St. Lawrence.

Cartier's eventual accounts of Hochelaga were probably exaggerated, but they succeeded in encouraging official backing of a full trading expedition to Hochelaga and 'Canada,' as the

Champlain provided the information for this representation of his battle against the Iroquois on Lake Champlain. He killed two of them and wounded a third with one blast of his arquebus, having loaded it with four balls.

NEW FRANCE

Before the arrival of white men, the country immediately north of the St. Lawrence was inhabited chiefly by scattered groups of Algonquian-speaking peoples — the Montagnais (or mountain-men) east of the St. Maurice river, and the Algonquins to the west.

These peoples were nomadic, and lived by hunting moose and other animals in the forest and spearing salmon and eels in the rivers and the sea. It was probably a group of Montagnais on a fishing expedition in the Bay of Gaspé who encountered Jacques Cartier and his French sailors in July 1534, when they landed and set up a cross on the shore.

That was the day Cartier took possession of the new territory in the name of the King of France, though he immediately re-embarked and soon returned to Europe. With him went two sons of the Montagnais chief, who in France learned enough of the ways of white men to act as interpreters when Cartier recrossed the ocean in 1535.

The Indians guided Cartier up the St. Lawrence to their settlement, Stadacona, opposite the Ile d'Orléans. They did all they could to persuade the white men to remain with them, but Cartier was determined to proceed farther up the river to a settlement he had evidently been told about — Hochelaga, on today's island of Montreal.

Judging from Cartier's description of Hochelaga's defences and 'long houses,'

English Privateers

Champlain's career in Quebec was not without problems. The fortunes of the little settlement were continually affected by political upheavals far away in France. But it seemed that prosperity was assured when, in 1627, the powerful Cardinal Richelieu backed the formation of the Company of One Hundred Associates.

The company was pledged to extend the realm of New France throughout North America, and in 1628 it launched a large convoy bound for Quebec and carrying both provisions and new settlers. Off the Gaspé the convoy was intercepted by English privateers led by the three Kirke brothers, and was captured intact.

The Kirkes ferried their booty to England, and returned to lay siege to Quebec itself the next year. They found Champlain and the colonists in pitiful condition. Champlain agreed to surrender the settlement on the condition that the Kirkes provided passage to Europe for all who wanted to go, including himself.

One of the Kirkes remained to hold Quebec. When the others reached home, they found that England and France had made peace only a month after they had left Europe, and that they were obliged to give up their conquests. Charles I demanded that they return all the booty captured in Quebec and from the convoy. The king's motivation was that France still owed him most of Queen Henrietta's dowry.

When the Kirkes refused to comply, not merely the haul from the convoy but also furs and other goods obtained elsewhere were seized by force. In 1632 Champlain returned to Quebec, as did the French flag.

A romantic presentation of the Kirke brothers' siege of Quebec in 1629.

French now termed the mainland. However, the venture turned sour when Cartier returned to France in 1542 with a worthless shipload of bogus minerals.

Official interest in Canada waned, though private adventurers launched more trading expeditions. In 1600 Pierre Chauvin, Sieur de Tonnetuit, of Dieppe, established a small trading post at Tadoussac, where the Saguenay river joins the St. Lawrence. A private expedition of 1603 included among its members the geographer Samuel de Champlain.

In 1608 Champlain was on the St. Lawrence once more, this time as lieutenant of a trading expedition launched by Pierre du Gua, Sieur de Monts. As his headquarters, Champlain selected the point of land termed 'Quebec' by the Indians — a natural rock citadel close to Stadacona and commanding a view of the St. Lawrence both upstream and downstream.

Champlain immediately ordered the construction of a wooden *habitation* two storeys high on the river bank. In the terms of its charter, the expedition was assured of no more than one year's trading. But judging from the scale of his operations, Champlain was confident that the French were in Canada for good.

The French leader was soon on friendly terms with local Indians. In 1609 they induced him to join in a raid against the troublesome Iroquois living south of the St. Lawrence, who were members of the great Confederacy of the Five Nations. Champlain and two other Frenchmen took with them their musketeer-style armour and arquebuses.

When the time came to attack, the Montagnais and Algonquins parted ranks and allowed Champlain to advance majestically forward towards the astonished Iroquois. He had loaded his arquebus with four balls, and when he fired, two Iroquois were killed and a third fell wounded.

The Iroquois stood still in disbelief until the two other Frenchmen appeared from the bushes. One of them fired, and the Iroquois fled with victorious Algonquins at their heels. A torture session that followed disgusted Champlain, but he was allowed to put the victim out of his misery.

The Iroquois never forgave the French for Champlain's participation or for his part in a similar action farther west in 1615 against the Onondagas. But at least he secured the full loyalty of Indians north of the St. Lawrence. When he died in Quebec in 1635, he was mourned as much by the Indians as by the white men who survived him.

Jacques Cartier visited Montreal island in 1535 and explored the settlement of Hochelaga, which was established there. This contemporary diagram illustrates the village's long houses and palisades, and the cultivated fields outside.

Quebec City's foundation was Champlain's *habitation*, built on the banks of the St. Lawrence where the church of Notre Dame des Victoires now stands.

Quebec City's golden years were in the seventeenth and early eighteenth centuries, the era of great governors like Tracy and Frontenac and of intendant Jean Talon. This is how Quebec appeared at the end of the seventeenth century.

THE GOVERNORS

Since the period of Champlain's forays against the Iroquois, Dutch traders on the Hudson river had equipped them with firearms to improve their hunting. The weapons helped their fighting too, and they returned to menace the peoples farther north. Most of their efforts were directed against the numerous Hurons of the west, who acted as entrepreneurs in carrying pelts from the interior to the French at Quebec.

In 1641 a group in Paris decided to establish a Jesuit mission for the Hurons on the island where Hochelaga had stood, known as Royal Mount or, as the French termed it, *Mont Réal*. The expedition was led by a career soldier, Paul de Chomedy, Sieur de Maisonneuve. With an assortment of followers including several missionaries, he landed on Montreal island in May 1642. They build a small palisaded settlement which they named 'Ville Marie,' and in gratitude for their success they later erected a huge cross on the mountain-top.

In 1643 a party of Huron converts, a missionary, and two other Frenchmen were ambushed by Iroquois as they

Situated at the point on the St. Lawrence where the river narrows, Quebec occupied a key defensive position. An anonymous painting from the time of Wolfe's siege of 1759 demonstrates the city's natural strength.

paddled up the St. Lawrence. The missionary was tortured, though with the help of Dutch traders he escaped death, but the Hurons were burned at the stake. A year later the missionary returned and was killed.

These incidents prefaced slowly worsening relations between the French and Iroquois, who soon drove the Hurons from their traditional trade routes, and in 1649–50 destroyed their power for good. The Iroquois took over the Hurons' place in the fur trade of the interior, carrying pelts not to the French but to the English farther south.

As a result many French settled at Montreal, which was at the confluence of the St. Lawrence and Ottawa rivers, the main arteries of commerce. Groups of French took to ambushing Iroquois canoes laden with pelts, their only means of sharing in the western trade. One such buccaneering expedition of 1660 was led by Adam Dollard des Ormeaux. On this occasion the French had miscalculated. The Iroquois had grown used to ambushes on the Ottawa and had taken to descending the river in

Trois Rivières was established by Champlain's order in 1634 as a fort and trading post, to accommodate Huron fur traders travelling from the interior. For the rest of the seventeenth century the settlement was the most important centre of the Quebec fur trade.

convoys. Dollard, sixteen French companions, and some Hurons and Algonquins took refuge in an old stockade, where they were besieged by the Iroquois until they were eventually overcome.

Further attacks and outrages convinced the authorities in France that decisive action was necessary if New France was to survive. In 1663 the Company of One Hundred Associates was relieved of its charter, and instead Canada became a Crown colony. To bolster its defences, Louis XIV sent out the famous Carignan-Salières regiment.

Besides the regiment, Louis and his minister, Jean Baptiste Colbert, appointed a succession of military governors and civil intendants. Two who arrived in 1665, Alexandre de Proville, Marquis de Tracy, as governor and Jean Talon as intendant, left an indelible impression — Tracy by waging a successful campaign against the Iroquois, and Talon by establishing a flourishing economy.

Louis de Buade, Comte de Frontenac, a new governor sent out from France in 1672, convened a great meeting of the western Iroquois at Cataraqui on Lake Ontario. To demonstrate French power to the warriors, he had a fort built and completed while the conference proceeded. Frontenac promised the Indians gifts from France in return for good behaviour.

But Frontenac's relations with others in New France — particularly with the church in general and with colonists in Montreal — were less than happy, and in 1682 he was recalled. His successors, Joseph Antoine Lefebvre de la Barre and Jacques René de Brisay, Marquis de Denonville, believed that the Iroquois were again disrupting the fur trade of the west. The French compaigned against them, forcing an uneasy peace.

When James II of England (a Catholic) was overthrown in 1689 by William and Mary (Protestants), war broke out between England and France. As allies of the English, the Iroquois swept down on the district of Lachine, killed 200 French, and captured many others. The French quickly reappointed Frontenac as governor, and he returned to Quebec.

Frontenac made peace with the Iroquois once more, and to impress them embarked on a series of raids against the settlements of New England. But in 1690 the tables were turned: an invasion fleet from New England swept up the St. Lawrence and demanded the surrender of Quebec.

Highly indignant, Frontenac refused. The New Englanders outnumbered the defenders, but their admiral (William Phips) misjudged his attack on the formidable fortress. His fleet was obliged to withdraw. As a souvenir the French recovered the flagship's ensign, knocked overboard by cannon fire and left floating in the water.

Public Archives Canada, C-30926

No portrait of Frontenac survives, but this amusing drawing shows him on his way to meet the Iroquois at Cataraqui in 1695. He is carried in a canoe by friendly Algonquin braves.

The Seigneuries

Jean Talon's brief was to encourage the clearing and cultivation of more land and to establish local industries. In support of this he was to found a series of settlements to build a sturdy colony. But when the intendant arrived he found that there were no more than 3000 colonists in all New France.

As a first step towards settling more territory, Talon offered large grants of land (manors or 'seigneuries') to officers of the Carignan-Salières regiment if they undertook to settle discharged veterans upon it. In the same way he offered land to persons of substance in the colony, if they promised to introduce new settlers.

Landholders, or seigneurs, swore loyalty to the king before the intendant, and signed a contract to maintain a manorhouse on the seigneury, to cede land to habitants (tenants), to build a flour mill, and perhaps to establish a court to settle local grievances. In return they received modest payments of rent, dues, and obligatory services from the habitants.

Habitants occupied rectangular allotments of land in the seigneury, each one about 1.6 km deep and about 60 m wide. A front rang or row of these strips normally followed a lake or river bank. Houses and farm buildings were built along a road through the seigneury, giving the impression of a continuous village street.

As a front rang filled up, further allotments were made in a second rang behind it. Thus married sons could open farms in the same seigneury as their father, and close family bonds developed between habitants of each locality. Further rangs were developed as needed, and some seigneuries came to include as many as ten.

From Quebec Talon turned to France and induced considerable immigration to the colony on promise of free passage and free land. There was a strong response from Normandy and the Ile de France. Many hundreds of 'King's Daughters' also made the crossing — orphans and the daughters of poor families destined to marry the settlers. As an inducement to marriage the adminstration provided wedding presents and relief from taxes.

Through these measures the population of New France more than doubled between 1665 and 1672. From 1675 there was little further immigration, and the families of New France increased its population unassisted.

Talon   **Laval**

A remarkable triumvirate governed Quebec in the 1670s — Governor Frontenac, Intendant Jean Talon, and Mgr. François de Laval, the bishop.

ADVENTURERS

Besides Quebec and Montreal there was a third important settlement in New France: Trois Rivières, where in 1634 Champlain ordered construction of a fort. He aimed to stamp out illegal fur trading and keep the Iroquois away from the Hurons and the Algonquins. The river delta had long been an important rendezvous in the fur trade, perhaps the most important, and so it continued. Hurons and other Indians arrived from the wilds until their trade patterns were disrupted by the Iroquois.

In the 1650s white men of Trois Rivières took to venturing into the interior on their own account. Among them were Pierre Radisson and his brother-in-law, Médard Chouart, Sieur des Groseilliers (a nickname meaning 'gooseberries'). The two made several journeys to the lands bordering Lakes Michigan and Superior, where they made contact with Hurons and Ottawas and found beaver pelts much heavier and thicker than any they had seen before.

D'Iberville's first expeditions against the English of the Hudson's Bay Company were made overland, but the last three were by sea. Here Inuit encountered in Hudson Bay assist the white men to secure D'Iberville's ship, the *Pelican*, for the winter months.

The two Frenchmen found the Indians ready to act as middlemen in trading with tribal hunters of the northwest. It is possible that they themselves reached the shores of Hudson Bay, but certainly they learned of its existence. In 1653 they descended the St. Lawrence with sixty canoes laden with pelts, which were promptly confiscated. It seems they had been refused permission to trade for pelts unless they agreed to share their profits with the governor. The two went to France to complain of the injustice but were shown no sympathy. In high dudgeon they went to England, where they outlined a grand scheme for reaching the fur lands through Hudson Bay.

They found an enthusiastic audience in Prince Rupert, a cousin of King Charles II, who persuaded friends to finance an exploratory expedition to Hudson Bay under the two Frenchmen. Radisson and the *Nonsuch* returned laden with furs, and in 1670 the king was induced to grant the charter which became the basis of the Hudson's Bay Company.

Meanwhile, other French adventurers were in the interior. In 1673 Frontenac sent Louis Jolliet, a fur trader, and the Jesuit Jacques Marquette to explore the west. They canoed down the Mississippi as far as the Arkansas river. In

1679 Jolliet explored the Saguenay and penetrated the Hudson Bay region.

In 1682 René Robert Cavalier, Sieur de LaSalle, pursued Jolliet's path down the Mississippi and reached the Gulf of Mexico. He named the enormous territory thus opened Louisiana, in honour of Louis XIV. But in leading an expedition to colonize the mouth of the Mississippi in 1684, LaSalle was murdered by mutineers among his followers.

Louisiana was eventually colonized in 1699 by Pierre Le Moyne, Sieur d'Iberville, who had been born in Montreal. Earlier, this same d'Iberville had invaded Newfoundland in 1696. His most famous ventures were five raids against posts of the Hudson's Bay Company, established at river mouths in Hudson Bay and James Bay. D'Iberville's first foray had taken him overland in 1685, under the command of Pierre, Chevalier de Troyes. They had seized three English posts on James Bay. D'Iberville remained to command them until 1687. His subsequent raids, all of which he commanded, were in 1688, 1690, 1694, and 1697. The last three were by sea.

D'Iberville's campaign was an effort to drive the English from the Bay, where the French insisted they had no right to be. It was unsuccessful. At one time or another the French held every one of the

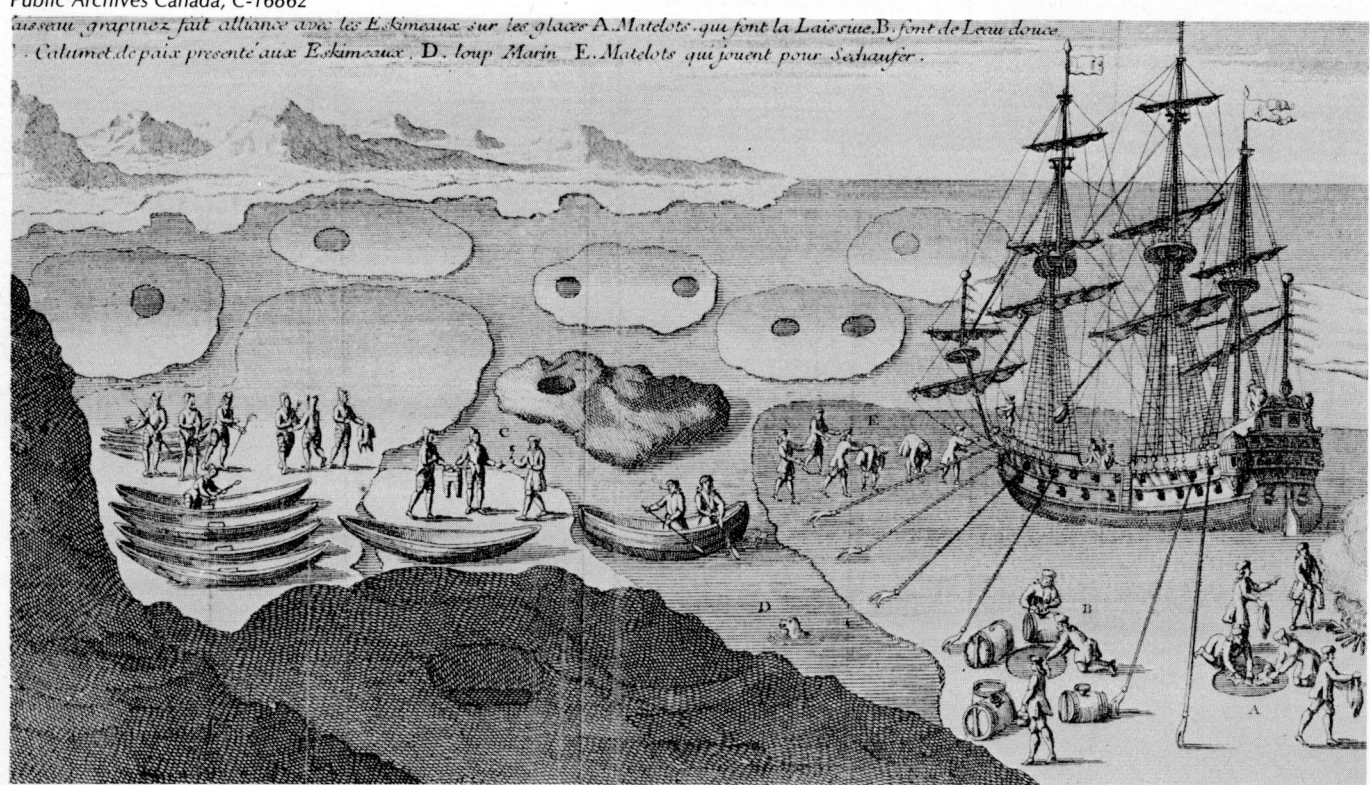

Public Archives Canada, C-1225

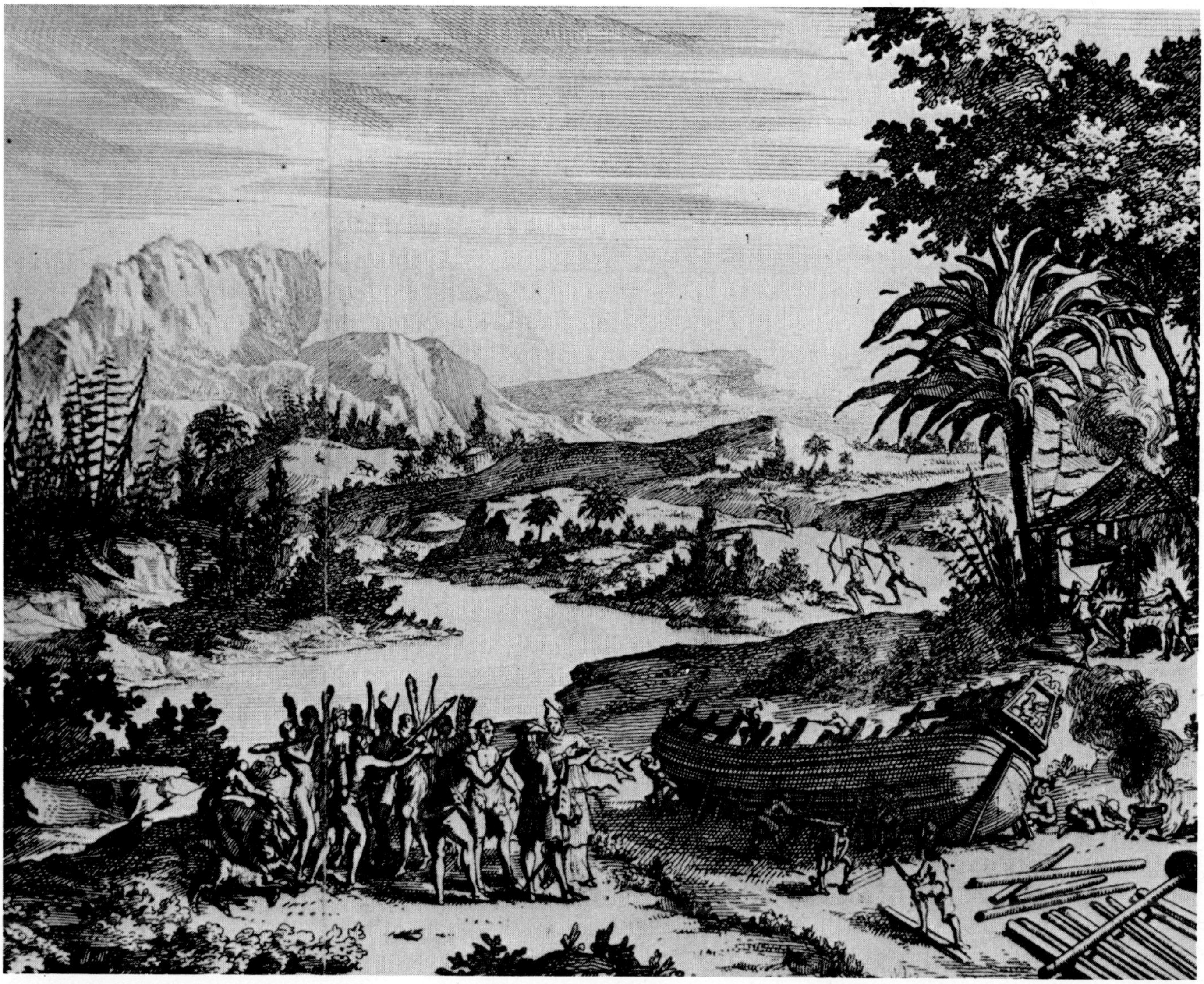

The first ship to be built on the Great Lakes was LaSalle's *Griffin*, completed in 1679 on Lake Erie. Laden with furs, she disappeared without trace when sailing on Lake Huron.

five English posts, though never all at once. By the Treaty of Utrecht of 1713, the French conceded to the English all of Rupert's Land — the vast area surrounding Hudson Bay.

The French had realized that the treaty would mean increased competition from the English in the fur trade, both from the north and from New England. To answer the twin challenges, they established a series of forts curving south down the Mississippi valley and another series towards the north-west.

In 1730 the French appointed Pierre Gaultier de Varennes, Sieur de la Vérendrye, of Trois Rivières, to command these western posts. He was instructed to concentrate on finding a route to the fabled western sea which led to China. He was to finance his explorations from the profits of the fur trade.

In the years that followed, La Vérendrye carried out his task, assisted by his four sons and a nephew. They first headed west, building forts as they went, and then north into the areas of present day Saskatchewan and Alberta, and finally south-west on a great journey which took them within sight of the Rocky Mountains.

Public Archives Canada, C-1349

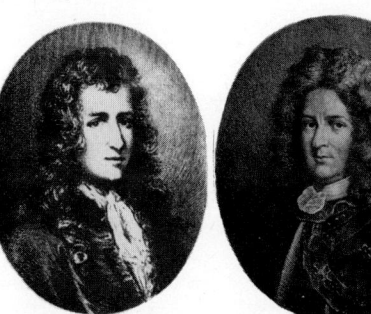

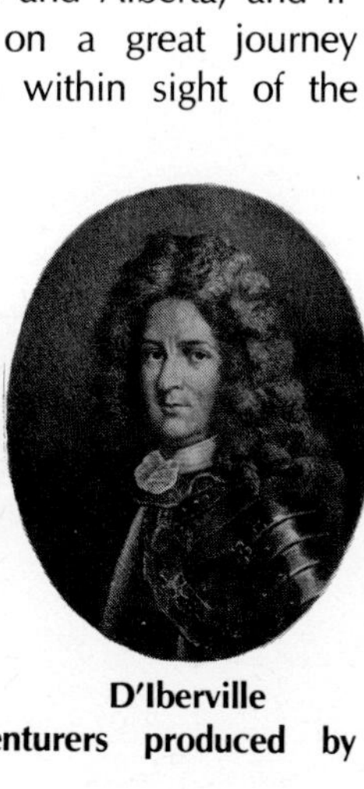

La Salle D'Iberville
The greatest adventurers produced by Quebec.

The former home of Louis Jolliet, off Place Royale in Quebec City, is now the lower station of a cable lift that carries passengers to the upper town.

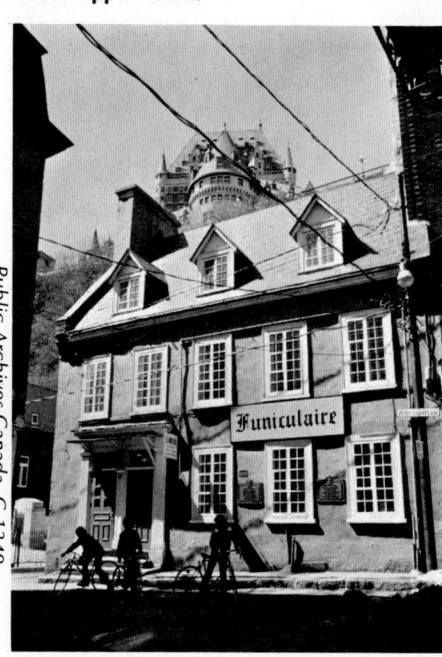

Wolfe's forces landed above Quebec early in the morning of September 13, 1759, and under cover of darkness ascended the cliffs of the Plains of Abraham, where they engaged in battle with the French.

WAR WITH ENGLAND

The first half of the eighteenth century was punctuated by a series of European wars that found England and France on opposite sides. Events were reflected in developments across the Atlantic and indeed around the world.

These culminated in the most serious of the conflicts, the Seven Years' War, which broke out in 1756. Britain was poorly prepared, but France was determined to press home its advantage in North America and despatched two fresh regiments to Quebec under the command of Louis Joseph, Marquis de Montcalm.

Montcalm's brief was to secure the southern frontier of New France and consolidate the new territory of Louisiana. In these years the English of the eastern seaboard had made vigorous efforts to move farther inland, in direct contravention of France's territorial claims to the Ohio valley.

Montcalm quickly captured two British forts and cleared the upper part of the Ohio valley, affording a passage to the strong Fort Duquesne farther south, which had been completed before his arrival. As his own base he fortified the post of Carillon, today's Ticonderoga, on the shores of Lake Champlain and commanding the route north.

At the outset of the war Montcalm found himself abandoned by France, where there had been a change of government. If he could hold out, well and good, but he could expect no more help. To add to his difficulties, he found New France in the hands of an autocratic governor, Pierre de Rigaud, Marquis de Vaudreuil, and a corrupt intendant, François Bigot.

Meanwhile, the English war effort came under the control of William Pitt, appointed secretary for war in 1757. Pitt was determined to foil French expansion in the Americas, and in 1758 he ordered a three-pronged campaign against Fort Duquesne, Montreal, and Louisbourg on Cape Breton Island.

James Wolfe was wounded twice during the short engagement with Montcalm's troops, and died on the field. He was buried in the church of St. Alphage, Greenwich, in London, England.

At Louisbourg the English were successful, and James Wolfe won distinction there. The English had to wait until fall to force the capitulation of Fort Duquesne, later renamed Pittsburgh in Pitt's honour. The invasion force destined for Montreal met Montcalm at Fort Carillon and was repulsed with heavy losses.

In 1759 Pitt tried once more. This time he aimed to take Fort Niagara, Montreal, and Quebec. Fort Niagara was won, largely through help from the Iroquois, but the force had no strength to continue on to Montreal. The British despatched to Quebec a large invasion fleet carrying an army commanded by James Wolfe.

By this time Montcalm had fallen back on Quebec because he was running short of supplies as a result of an Atlantic blockade by the English. The British bombarded the city for weeks, and not one structure escaped damage. An attempted landing on the Beauport shore was foiled when the boats carrying the British ran aground.

With the summer drawing to a close, Wolfe decided on one final attack. He created two diversions — a bombardment opposite Montcalm's headquarters downstream, and a long chase upstream as French troops pursued a British flotilla threatening to land. This absented more than 2000 defenders from the main force.

Wolfe himself remained near Quebec. With about 4000 men he sailed silently to a passage up a cliff a short distance above the city, leading to the Plains of Abraham. There, at dawn, the British overcame two small French posts and moved on to take up a strong position before the walls of Quebec.

Montcalm moved quickly, and marched regular troops to confront Wolfe's men. But Governor Vaudreuil, technically his superior, failed to comply with requests for support. The French advanced in their customary tight-packed formation, which was six men deep. The British has formed a thin red line, devised by Wolfe, which extended over a wide front and was forbidden to shoot until the French were close. At last the British fired three volleys. The French line was routed, and the British chased the broken regiments towards the walls of Quebec.

Wolfe had been fatally wounded, but died knowing that his strategy had worked. Montcalm had been seriously wounded too, and died in Quebec the next day. The British camped outside the walls and formally demanded the city's surrender.

However, much of the French army escaped and joined François Gaston, Duc de Lévis, at Montreal. Next spring Lévis marched on Quebec, and in April the French defeated the British at Ste.

Foy near the city. The British withdrew into Quebec and were besieged, but were rescued when English ships arrived with reinforcements and supplies.

The French were driven back to Montreal, where the British army joined two other friendly forces from the Richelieu and Lake Ontario. In September 1760 Governor Vaudreuil surrendered New France without further struggle.

Montcalm　　　　Wolfe

Twin heroes of the battle for Quebec.

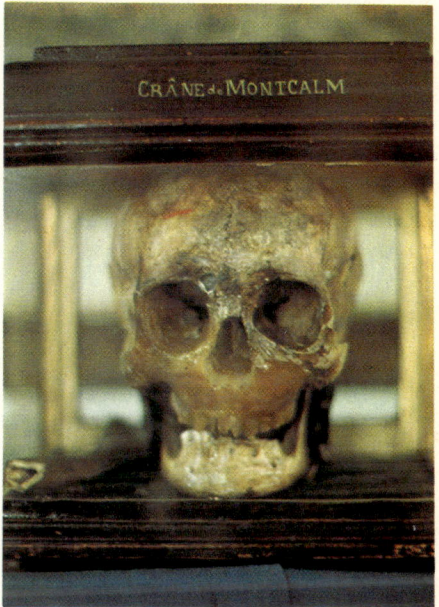

The relics of Montcalm, his skull and a bone, are preserved at the Convent of the Ursulines in Quebec City.

Built to commemorate Quebec's victory over New England in 1695, Notre Dame des Victoires in Place Royal was destroyed during the British bombardment of 1759. It was subsequently rebuilt.

REBELLION

At the end of the Seven Years' War, a small party in England wanted to return Quebec to France in exchange for the West Indian island of Guadeloupe. It believed that a French presence in Canada was desirable as a check on the ambitions of British colonies to the south.

The British government did not agree. Instead, a full-fledged British administration was installed at Quebec, at first committed to anglicizing the French as quickly as possible. However, Sir Guy Carleton, the governor sent out in 1764, realized that such a policy was unworkable and allowed things to continue as before.

In 1774 the status quo was enshrined in the Quebec Act. It proclaimed an extension of Quebec's borders (hemming in the northernmost of the 'English' colonies). It also gave full authority to the Roman Catholic church, maintained the seigneurial landlord system, and provided for civil justice under 'the laws of Canada' — in fact, French law.

The provisions incensed the representatives of the English colonies, to whom the Quebec Act was perhaps the worst of George III's 'intolerable acts,' particularly in its limitation of their borders. A deputation including Benjamin Franklin was despatched to woo the French Canadians into demanding representative government. However its appeals fell on deaf ears. There had been grumbles from the habitants about the need to pay tithes and rents. But the establishment — the churchmen and the landlords — was happy with the new arrangements. When the American War of Independence broke out, the revolutionaries of the south attempted to seize Canada by force.

The Americans took Ticonderoga in May 1775, and in November a force under Richard Montgomery forced Montreal to capitulate. Governor Carleton narrowly escaped capture. Montgomery's force joined another party led by Benedict Arnold at Quebec in December, but in their first attack on the city Montgomery was fatally wounded. The Americans settled down to besiege Quebec, and there they remained until spring, when a British fleet arrived with

The rebellion of 1837 and 1838 saw several battles between French Canadian *Patriotes* and British troops. Here the British attack insurgents in the village of St. Charles in November 1837.

General Richard Montgomery of the United States was killed leading an attack on Quebec City in December 1775, during the American War of Independence. American troops under Benedict Arnold besieged the city throughout the winter, but when a relief force was defeated at Trois Rivières the next spring, the Americans returned to the south.

In December 1837 British troops dispersed French Canadian Patriotes in the village of St. Eustache, near Montreal.

16

reinforcements. By this time the Americans had lost what little respect and sympathy they had enjoyed in Quebec, and in spite of French support of the revolution, the Canadians remained loyal to King George.

At this time a number of British and American traders, who had been based at Albany in New York, moved to Montreal. These and other new settlers pressed the authorities to introduce representative government. There were similar agitations elsewhere in the British colonies, particularly west of the Ottawa river.

In response, the British government passed the Constitutional Act of 1791, which divided Quebec into two provinces, Upper and Lower Canada, west and east of the Ottawa. It provided them with nominated legislative councils and elected assemblies, like those which had existed in the English colonies. The first election was held in 1792.

Elected government was a novelty to the French Canadians, who had never known democracy and who had been shielded from the French Revolution of 1789. Strangely, the revolution encouraged the British authorities to allow French Canadians greater freedom to develop their own culture, and particularly their religion.

Before, the British had been skeptical of the Roman Catholic church's activities, and churchmen from France had been banned. Now, as many were admitted as cared to come. However, following Lower Canada's survival of the War of 1812, from which it was largely protected by British victories in Upper Canada, there was a growing demand for more rights. Heading the movement was Louis Joseph Papineau, who led the French-speaking majority in the legislative assembly. He demanded that the English *château clique*, which made up the governor's council, should be subject to election like the assembly. In 1834 he and his associates issued a long list of grievances (the ninety-two resolutions) from which they demanded redress.

The demands were so extreme that Papineau lost the support of many of his own associates, and also that of leaders of the church. In 1837 the British passed 'ten resolutions,' expressly refusing to contemplate elections to the council and empowering it to raise and spend money without the consent of the assembly.

The same year crops failed and unemployment spread. General unrest worried the English in Montreal, and some of them clashed with young French *Patriotes* in a Montreal street. Soon a general insurrection broke out. *Patriote* irregulars fought British troops in battles at St. Charles and St. Eustache near Montreal. In spite of bad feeling, the upheavals led to major legislative changes in 1841.

Responsible Government

Following the 1837 rebellions in both Lower and Upper Canada, the British appointed Lord Durham as governor-general of the provinces and colonies in British North America. In Lower Canada many leaders of the 1837 rebellion had been condemned to death, but Durham banished some to another colony and freed others with a caution.

Durham had no clear right to interfere, however, and after heavy attacks in the British House of Commons he resigned and returned home. Within two months he and two collaborators produced a *Report on the Affairs of British North America*, which proposed that the two Canadas be united and granted responsible government.

One of Durham's aims in making these recommendations was to ensure that the French of Lower Canada were quickly anglicized, for he noted that as things stood their language was a major barrier and would inevitably penalize them. In 1841 the British government passed an Act of Union, which produced a united Canada.

Quebec was now known as Canada East, while Upper Canada became Canada West. Each sent an equal number of representatives to the elected assembly, but under the terms of the Act of Union the governor was not responsible to the assembly, but to the Colonial Office in London. Members of the assembly, whether English or French, continued to bridle.

Then, in 1846, the Whigs returned to power in England, and Durham's son-in-law, Lord Elgin, was sent to the Canadas as governor-general. He was in favour of responsible government. When the 'Reform Party' came into power in both parts of the province, he called on Robert Baldwin of Canada West and Louis LaFontaine of Canada East, an old associate of Papineau's, to form a ministry.

In 1849 Elgin sanctioned the Rebellion Losses Bill recommended by this ministry, which was designed to compensate anyone in Canada East whose property had been damaged through the events of 1837 and 1838. The move infuriated English merchants of Montreal, who saw it as one more move to bolster the French, and they burned down the parliament buildings.

Durham

Elgin

Lord Durham and Lord Elgin, father-in-law and son-in-law, brought responsible government to Quebec.

Papineau

LaFontaine

Joseph Papineau and Louis LaFontaine were among the leaders of Quebec's reform movement.

Public Archives Canada, C-16751

17

Krieghoff's famous painting of a group of habitants playing cards, c. 1860.

THE PARISHES

The early decades of the nineteenth century saw large-scale immigration to the Canadas from the British Isles and the United States. Most of the new arrivals headed west of the Ottawa river, but many remained in Lower Canada.

English-speaking newcomers settled in the Eastern Townships surveyed for them south of the St. Lawrence, on land behind the seigneuries, running to the American border. Land lots were divided by the British system — five-sevenths granted to settlers and two-sevenths reserved for Protestant clergy to pay for churches, schools, and hospitals.

By the 1840s the English-speaking population of Lower Canada made up one-fifth of the whole. It was located mainly in the Eastern Townships and Montreal, which was now booming as a commercial centre. The French majority lived in Quebec, Trois Rivières, Montreal, and on the seigneurial tenures both north and south of the St. Lawrence.

Over the years each district had built a church to serve habitants in local seigneuries, their priests supported by tithes of one-twenty-fifth of the production of each family unit. The church became a natural focus and often a village developed around it. Ultimately congregations elected parish councils to oversee both religious and civic affairs.

But in many areas, land available in seigneuries was now fully occupied. It had been the tradition for sons in a family to take up land behind their father's, clearing it of trees and developing it to support a family of their own. But with no land available, family members were leaving for other areas. In the eyes of the church this meant a serious disruption of the community. Thus, from the 1850s the church initiated colonization societies, which bought land in the Townships and also north of the St. Lawrence. In each location a church was built as the centre

of a parish, and prospective habitants built log cabins and cleared the wilderness.

Eventually the French-speaking population of the Townships came to outnumber the English-speaking, partly because many of the original anglophone settlers sold their homes and moved west. As in the seigneuries, habitants paid tithes to the church to support the local priest, who was in every sense the leader of the community.

The agricultural tradition of Lower Canada's society was preserved, but to an increasing extent new industries were developed. There was wood-cutting in the St. Maurice and Richelieu river valleys, and later farther upstream on the Ottawa, and lumber was exported to Europe from Quebec City. Many habitant farmers doubled as lumbermen during winter months.

Montreal and Quebec thrived as commercial centres, particularly Mont-

Rows of seigneurial farms fronted the river, and narrow parallel strips of cultivated land extended about 1.6 km into the hinterland. When the front row was full, more farms were developed in rows behind them.

real, since it was the last port of significance before the St. Lawrence rapids, where imported goods for the interior were unloaded. Riverboats and other craft manned by Lower Canada's famous voyageurs ferried the goods upstream by a series of canals.

In 1845 a coalition party came into power in the two Canadas: the Liberal-Conservatives, led by Upper Canada's John A. Macdonald and George-Etienne Cartier, moderate reformer of Lower Canada. One of their first decisions was to secularize the Protestant clergy reserves both east and west of the Ottawa river.

They also abolished the seigneurial system, compensating landlords and allowing habitants to buy or rent their land directly from the province. However, communities of the Roman Catholic church were exempted from this measure, in view of their invaluable social work and their role in binding together the community. As the church held one-quarter of all seigneurial land and much in the Townships, that left much of rural society in the position it had always occupied. Local parish priests' influence remained strong, their bishops had a major say at government level, and in the 1860s the church supported moves towards confederating all the provinces of British North America.

Cornelius Krieghoff painted this *Farmhouse at Ste. Anne de Beaupré,* on the St. Lawrence close to Quebec City. Notice the trap door to a stone cellar, in which vegetables could be kept fresh.

Inns and taverns were important social centres throughout early Quebec. This is A. S. Gifford's painting of the *Inn at Jolifou.*

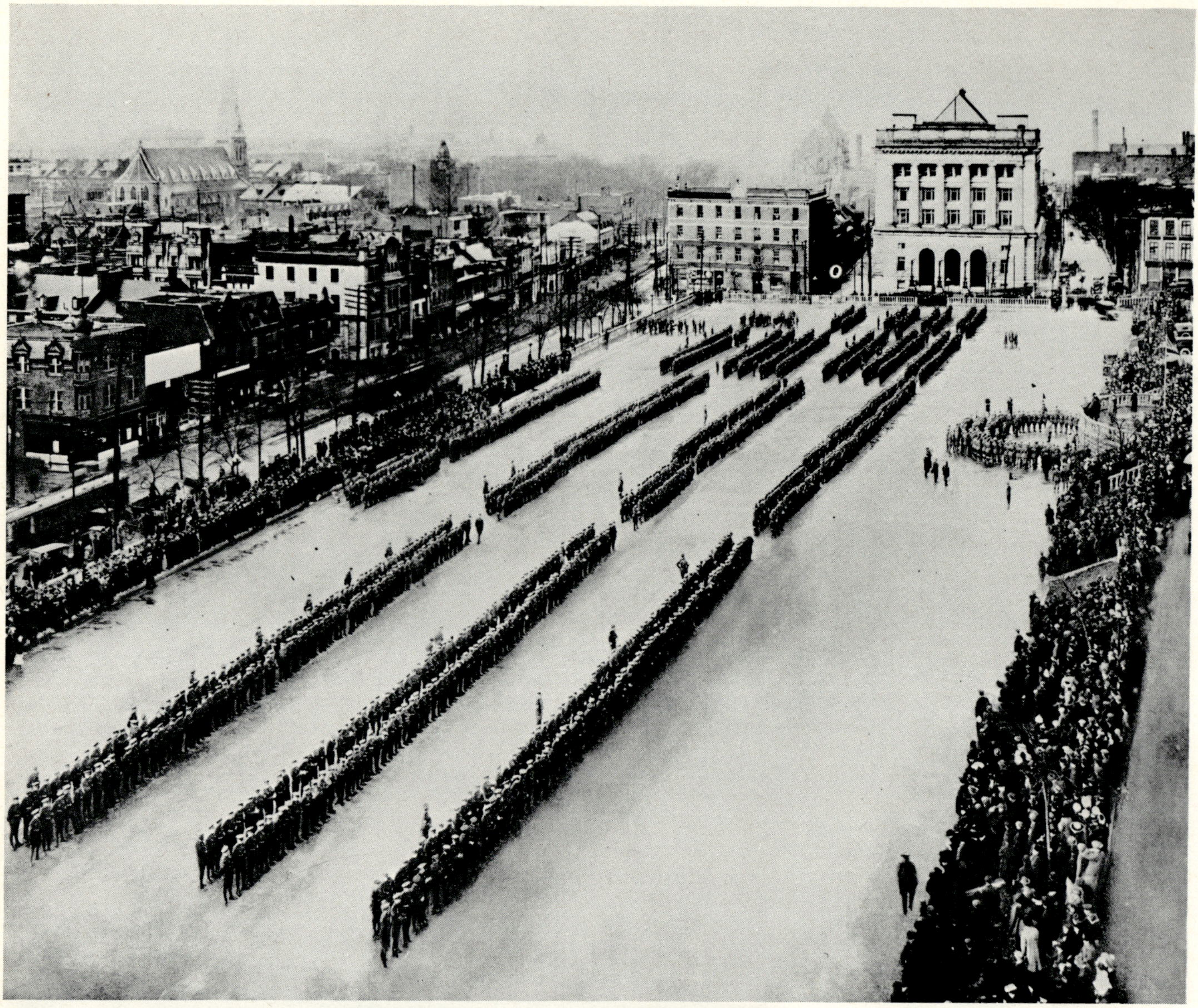

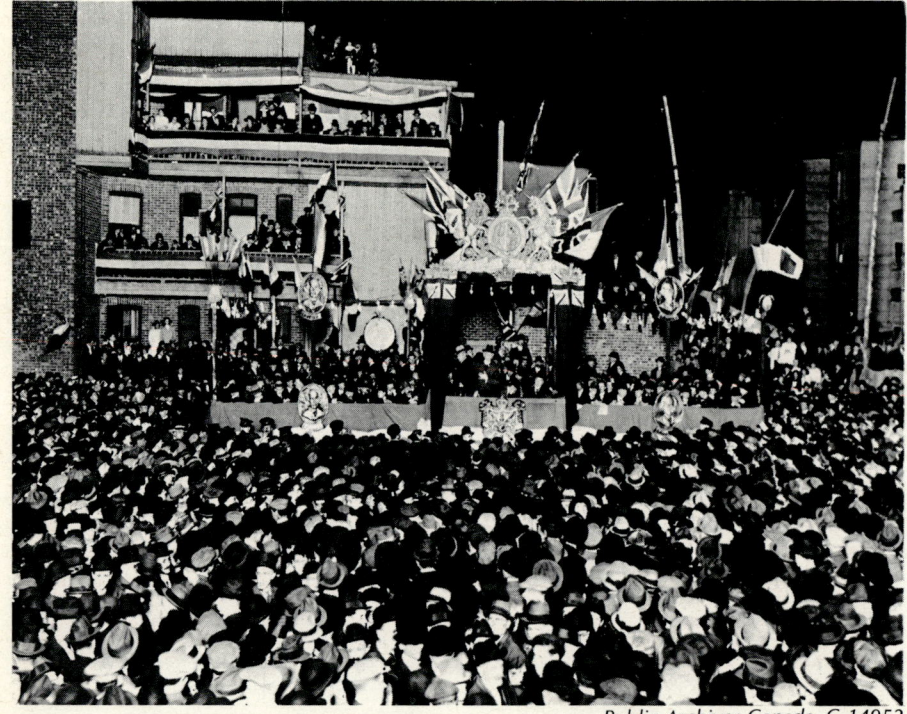

Canada's only regular francophone regiment, the Royal 22nd (Van Doos), parades in Montreal before leaving for France during World War I.

Public Archives Canada, C-14952

Sir Wilfrid Laurier addresses Montrealers during the early stages of World War I, encouraging them to enlist. However, most Quebeckers believed that the war was Europe's concern, not Canada's.

CONSCRIPTION

The British North America Act of 1867 enshrined French as an official language. Canada East became the Province of Quebec, with its own provincial government, which had far-reaching responsibilities in social and civil affairs.

For several decades it seemed that French Canadians were happy with the arrangement. Certainly few complained, though this was through respect for the church, which still wielded great authority. In fact, however, there was widespread poverty, the result of a swiftly increasing birthrate which the rural society could not absorb.

Through the 1880s and 1890s there was a steady drift to the cities, where many of the established English-speaking merchants took advantage of cheap labour to promote low-cost, labour-intensive industries. Even this market was soon glutted, and many French left Canada altogether to seek new opportunities in the United States.

But the French profile in Canada remained generally high, particularly when Wilfrid Laurier was prime minister of Canada. His Liberals won power in 1896, and to encourage national unity, Laurier introduced provincial statesmen from across Canada into his cabinet. He remained in power until 1911, and in that time helped to establish a Canadian presence in the world.

His successor, Robert Borden of the Conservatives, took Canada into World War I and committed the Canadian Corps of volunteers to the war effort. The cabinet decided to keep the force up to full strength. This meant that it was repeatedly called on to perform exacting assignments, and casualty levels stayed high.

In Quebec there were mixed feelings about the war, particularly since Henri Bourassa and the Nationalistes said that it was Europe's concern and had nothing to do with Canada. When Borden ordered conscription of childless males to reinforce the ailing Canadian corps, there was general dismay in Quebec and an immediate political crisis.

The outcry was not confined to Quebec, for there were serious misgivings throughout Canada. But in Quebec there was deep resentment that Quebeckers were being forced out of

The Van Doos entrain for the western front in 1915.

the country to fight 'England's war' and perhaps die in the process. There were riots, and English Canada poured scorn on Quebeckers' supposed lack of patriotism.

Borden was obliged to call an election at the end of 1917. By extending the franchise and by joining forces with English Liberals to form a union government, he retained power. But in Quebec, Laurier's French Liberals swept the board and took Quebec into opposition. There was a widening political gulf between the two language groups.

In the event, few conscripts, whether English or French, were actually sent to Europe. English and French Liberals reunited, but francophone resentment of the English survived. In 1936 a new political party came to power in Quebec's provincial legislature, and it was pledged to introduce a socialist society. The newcomer was the Union Nationale, which soon fell under the control of Maurice Duplessis. Ironically, Duplessis quickly steered the party caucus towards a policy directly opposed to its election platform — right-wing support of free enterprise and the church — though it remained committed to promoting Quebec nationalism.

Duplessis was thwarted in the provincial election of 1939, when federal cabinet ministers from Quebec campaigned against his effort to break Confederation. They promised that there would be no conscription if Canada went to war. The next year Mackenzie King called a federal election, and his government was voted in with an increased mandate.

One of the first acts of the new government was to introduce a measure giving it wide powers over people and property, including the right to conscript men for service within Canada, though explicitly ruling out call-up

for overseas duty. But in 1942 King called on Canadians to release him from the promises of no overseas conscription.

The resulting referendum revealed overwhelming approval in English Canada, but less than one-third support in Quebec. King did what he could to play down the issue, but in 1944 the forces' manpower shortage was so great that King could hold back no longer. He ordered conscription of 16 000 home-service recruits to Europe.

French Quebeckers disapproved, though not so severely as in 1917 because the federal government had done what it could to respect their views. Once more the end of the war meant that few conscripts actually went to Europe. However, the upset was sufficient to return the Union Nationale to power in 1944.

Laurier   **Bourassa**

The Conscription crisis of World War I pitted two great Quebeckers against each other — the patriot Henri Bourassa and the statesman Wilfrid Laurier.

THE ECONOMY

After five years out of office, Maurice Duplessis and the Union Nationale returned to power in 1944 and retained undisputed control over Quebec until the premier's sudden death in 1959. These years shaped the economic trends which linger to the present.

Duplessis — *le chef*, as Quebeckers knew him — believed that to survive, Quebeckers should remain true to their traditions. He identified these as a culture founded in religion and an economy founded in agriculture, and set out to strengthen the position of the Roman Catholic church and to deter industrial expansion in Quebec.

These policies had several significant effects. In the first place, francophone schools and universities were supervised by the church, and offered courses in the humanities rather than in science and economics. Francophones were denied any chance of real business education unless they attended English institutions.

In the second place, the English of Montreal were firmly entrenched and formed a natural plutocracy that was penetrated by very few francophone families. The presence of British investment had been prominent in Quebec since the days of the fur trade. Now it flourished since Duplessis discouraged American interference, which was making deep inroads elsewhere in Canada.

The birth rate was high, but there were few jobs in rural areas. This ensured a huge labour pool for manufacturing industries in Montreal and other centres. Isolated from American know-how, these industries were mostly labour-intensive, producing semi-durable goods for the consumer market.

It was left to Ontario — originally far behind Quebec in economic development — to establish capital-intensive industries. Except in pulp and paper, Quebec made no significant progress towards diversifying into heavy industry until the late 1950s.

Two brief Union Nationale governments succeeded Duplessis's, but in 1960 it was the turn of the Liberals under Jean Lesage. Though initially occupied with social reform, the Liberals soon turned their attention to economic matters. In 1962 Lesage's minister of

▲
Iron ore mines of the Labrador trench have provided the Quebec economy with major new impetus, though much of the iron ore produced is exported unbeneficiated. This is a mine at Schefferville, near the Quebec–Labrador boundary.

Chicoutimi is on the Saguenay fiord, and marks the highest point at which the river is navigable. It is the commercial centre of a region that supports mixed farming and forestry, and major heavy industrial enterprises, including aluminum smelting. ▼

Construction proceeds on LG 3, one of the four generating stations that make up the La Grande hydroelectric program. The main dam is on the south arm of the river.

James Bay

At Confederation Quebec occupied only a quarter of its present territory north and south of the St. Lawrence. Its vast northern wilderness was still part of Rupert's Land, the huge concession granted to the Hudson's Bay Company in 1670. In 1870 the company transferred Rupert's Land and the North West Territory to Canada.

In 1898 Rupert's Land east of James Bay was divided three ways among Quebec (the south), Newfoundland (the Labrador coast), and the Northwest Territories (the Ungava Peninsula). All were administered by the federal government. In 1912 the Northwest Territories east of Hudson Bay were transferred to Quebec.

In 1927 the British Privy Council decided a boundary dispute between Canada and Newfoundland (at the time not yet within Confederation) over Labrador. The present boundary follows the line of high mountain peaks forming a watershed, but recent Quebec governments have refused to accept the validity of the Privy Council's ruling.

The government of Jean Lesage was the first to look towards the rich natural resources of New Quebec. Several major projects have been launched, notably through the creation of the James Bay Development Corpo-

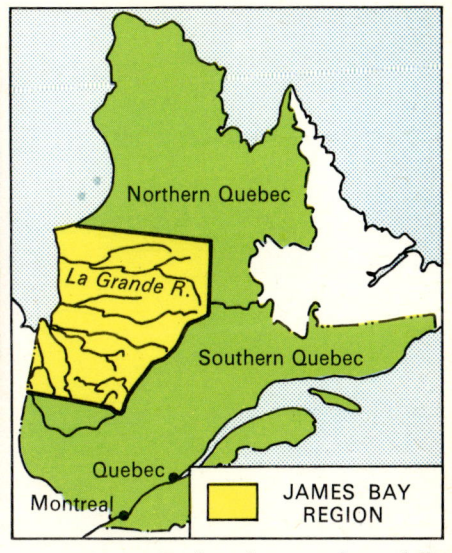

As yet New Quebec has not been fully explored, let alone developed. But a start has been made in the James Bay region. The La Grande hydroelectric scheme, mining, and forest harvesting are under way.

ration in 1971. The corporation coordinates development projects in the south-western portion of the region.

James Bay's resources include hydraulic power, minerals, forest products, and tourist appeal. Hydroelectric resources are being developed by the James Bay Energy Corporation on behalf of Hydro-Quebec, and focus on the La Grande river system. Mine and forest industries are being developed and add a key dimension to Quebec's economic prospect.

natural resources, René Lévesque, called for nationalization of most of the electricity industry. This was the first step in a campaign to win economic independence for Quebec. The financiers of Montreal's St. James Street, the heart of the business district, opposed it, but ordinary Quebeckers were enthusiastic. In 1965 Lévesque's ministry established a provincial mining company to explore and develop Quebec's mineral resources.

Meanwhile American capital poured into Quebec, as it did everywhere else in Canada. With it came American cultural influence, which increased Quebeckers' expectations of a high standard of living. However, English-speaking citizens remained in firm control of the big corporations' headquarters in Montreal, and ultimately of Quebec.

Indeed, it became plain through the 1960s and 1970s that the English had no intention of handing over to the French. Few francophones were promoted to executive status, and most of these were products of an English education. Successive provincial governments became increasingly irritated by the lack of progress.

From the mid-1970s the Liberal government and then the Parti Québécois, elected in 1976, used the French language as a lever to displace the English language in Quebec's economic life. Unfortunately the move accelerated a trend in which English companies relocated their headquarters outside Quebec, particularly in and near Toronto.

The Parti Québécois proposed to go further by taking Quebec out of Confederation, provided that suitable economic

interdependence with the rest of Canada could be maintained. Leaders in other provinces made it plain that such a scheme would not be acceptable.

Population

According to the Statistics Canada mini-census of 1976, the population of Montreal's metropolitan area (2 802 845) was only slightly smaller than the Toronto area's (2 803 101). However, as a city Montreal held 1 080 546 people compared with Toronto's 633 318.

Other metropolitan populations in Quebec are as follows:

Quebec City	542 158
Hull	171 947
Chicoutimi—Jonquière	128 643

In earlier days Quebec's population was chiefly rural, and villages tend to follow old seigneurial roads. This is the village of Les Eboulements, near Baie St. Paul on the north shore of the St. Lawrence — so named because of devastating landslides (*éboulements*) caused by a major earthquake in the Saguenay region in 1663.

AGRICULTURE

Farms in Quebec fall into three main categories: there are the old-style seigneurial allotments along rivers; there are English-style farms in the Eastern Townships; and there are pioneer enterprises in such regions as the Saguenay and Abitibi.

The old-style seigneurial divisions are still evident throughout southern Quebec, particularly along the St. Lawrence from Montreal to Rivière du Loup and south on the Richelieu river. But their traditional dimensions mean that single units are too small to be worked at a reasonable profit.

Before World War II, families living on these small farms were content to live at subsistence level, rotating such crops as hay, oats, barley, and wheat, and keeping cows for milk (though only in summer) and perhaps other animals.

The typical farm in Quebec is relatively small, though many farmers have taken over neighbouring farms to make their units more productive. This farm is at St. Ours on the Richelieu river.

Implements were horsedrawn, and the farmer depended on his family to labour in the fields.

Attitudes changed with the war. Country folk had more contact with the world outside and asked for improvements. Agricultural credit became more generally available, farmers turned to tractors and electricity, and many of the more enterprising bought out their neighbours in the interests of improving productivity.

Already youngsters were leaving farms in great numbers and heading for the cities in hopes of higher rewards and greater excitement. According to the 1941 census, 25 per cent of Quebec's population lived on farms. By 1971 the proportion was down to less than 6 per cent, and today it is smaller still.

At the same time the average age of farmers in Quebec has risen to older than fifty years. This is partly because farmers live longer than they used to, but it is also because eldest sons no longer automatically take over the family farm as in the past. The province has a serious shortage of young farmers.

Of course, these patterns chiefly affect small seigneurial-style farms which have not kept pace with technological development. The situation in the Townships and in other regions south of the St. Lawrence is less serious because soils are relatively more fertile, climate is more favourable, and farm layout is more efficient.

In the pioneer regions farther north, farms tend to be larger still. This is particularly the case in the Saguenay, settled in the 1850s and now famous for mixed farming. Large farms in the Abitibi region originating from the 1920s specialize in raising beef.

In all, only 10 per cent of Quebec's total land surface is arable. The chief farming districts are the St. Lawrence lowlands, the Laurentian plateau, and the Appalachian region. The most prosperous farms are those within reach of Montreal and its big markets, which cater to half of Quebec's population. Regions like Montreal Island, and such regions as Huntingdon and Ste. Hyacinthe south of Montreal support a wide range of enterprises. These include fruit and vegetable farming, dairy and beef production, and a number of special ventures like sugar beet growing.

Some farms are relatively isolated during the long months of winter, but radio and television help to relieve the loneliness.

Sugar beets are farmed in counties around Ste. Hyacinthe, and are shipped to the provincially owned sugar refinery at St. Hilaire to be processed.

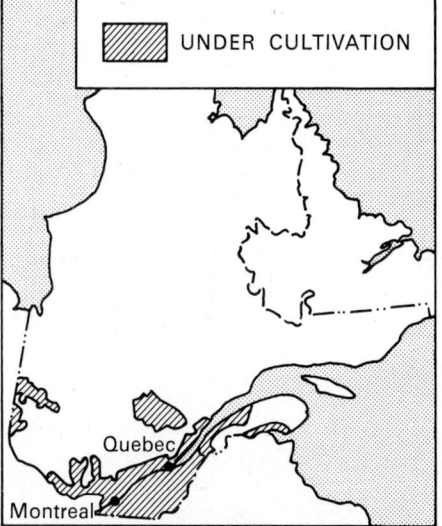

Only a tiny proportion of Quebec's vast land area is under cultivation. The most significant agricultural regions lie near the St. Lawrence river and in the Eastern Townships.

Louis Hébert

Quebec's first farmer was a Parisian apothecary, Louis Hébert, recruited by Champlain in 1616 to act as physician and surgeon to the colonists of New France. Champlain had met Hébert through the ill-fated first colonization of the Annapolis Basin (Nova Scotia), where the apothecary had grown herbs as the basis of his medications.

Hébert had also grown vegetables, and Champlain hoped that he would use his green thumb to similar effect in New France. The lands of the St. Lawrence were not nearly as fertile as Acadia, though local Indians had already demonstrated that agriculture was possible. Crops included corn and peas.

Hébert and his wife, son, and two daughters landed at Tadoussac in 1617, and farmed there and later in Quebec and north on the St. Charles river. The family cultivated corn, winter wheat, and other crops and introduced cattle, swine, and fowl. The colony's backers insisted that Hébert surrender his surplus production to the other colonists without payment.

Until the 1950s Ayrshire cows made up the majority of Quebec's dairy herd. They have since been overtaken by the Holstein, and today Ayrshires make up no more than twenty per cent of the total herd.

The upper Saguenay river valley provides some of Quebec's most attractive farm scenery, though flatter regions farther south are more fertile. ▼

DAIRY PRODUCE

There are some 27 000 milk producers in Quebec, out of a total of 60 000 agricultural producers counted in the 1971 census. In 1977 the province's combined dairy herd consisted of some 900 000 cows, but it is being substantially reduced.

Milk production has been a staple of Quebec agriculture since the earliest days. Samuel de Champlain imported the forerunners of the black Canadian breed between 1608 and 1610, and early inhabitants made butter, cheese, cream, and other products. However, cows were milked only in summer months when forage and grain feed were abundant.

In winter, cows were kept in barns and fed only forage. Quebec's habitants remained loyal to the Canadian breed, which had become hardy and able to stand Canada's difficult winters. But in the mid-nineteenth century the government of Canada imported brown-and-white Ayrshires that it thought would produce more milk.

Ayrshires held priority in Quebec until the 1950s, largely because of generous government subsidies in the early decades of the century. When the subsidies were discontinued, individual farmers turned to the Holstein, the black-and-white breed originally from the Netherlands which had been introduced to Quebec in 1885. The Holstein produces more milk than the Ayrshire, and the breed has become so popular that today it accounts for 75 per cent of Quebec's dairy herd. Ayrshires account for 20 per cent and Canadians for three per cent. The diminutive brown Jersey, noted for the high butterfat content of its milk, makes up a further 2 per cent.

A typical dairy herd in Quebec consists of fifty to sixty head, of which thirty would be producing cows. At the end of May or thereabouts (depending on the locality), the farmer puts his cows out to pasture. Forage crops provide 75 to 80 per cent of their energy requirements, though supplementary grain is fed to them at milking time.

The producing cows are milked twice a day, in a barn which serves as their home throughout winter. A few farms still use old-fashioned milking techniques, but most are automated. Since the early 1970s it has been technically obligatory for Quebec farmers to store milk in a bulk tank, and this is filled by a pipeline from the milking machines.

From October the cows spend all their time in the barn. They are fed dried forage (probably grown on the farm) and a mix of grain usually bought from outside producers. Cows are taken off milk production in rotation, to calve and keep up the strength of the herd. Fifty per cent of calving is the result of artificial insemination.

Milk from the farms is collected for two purposes — natural milk production, which involves pasteurization for fresh milk consumption, and industrial milk production, when it is converted into butter, cheese, cream, powdered milk, and other products. About 5000 dairy farmers concentrate on natural milk production, while the remainder focus on the industrial product.

Though dairy herds are found throughout the province, the best are concentrated in the centre, particularly in the region of Ste. Hyacinthe and Plessisville. Breeders compete at twenty regional fairs held throughout the province. There is a provincial fair each year in Quebec City, and champions compete in the Royal Winter Fair in Toronto.

Dairy production is the most important element in Quebec agriculture. In round figures it accounts for 40 per cent of farm receipts from animal production, which in turn accounts for about 80 per cent of total farm receipts in Quebec. However, it has been evident that there has been overproduction, at least on a regional basis, and the provincial government has urged farmers to prune herds and diversify.

Throughout winter, dairy cows are housed in clean, warm barns regularly checked for hygiene by government inspectors. The cows are fed a balanced diet of dried forage and grain feed.

The Canadian breed is little known today, but for centuries it was the most significant in Quebec.

Meat and Poultry

Dairy farming is the most valuable sector of Quebec agriculture, with swine production in second place. The province has 12 000 swine producers, 600 of them running specialist 'farrow-to-finish' operations which fatten the swine from birth until ready for slaughter.

Many of the specialist operations are located near Quebec City and in the Beauce farther south, within easy reach of grain supplies brought to Quebec City from Canada's western provinces. Favourite swine breeds are the York and Landrace. The animals are raised in clean, well-lit barns under controlled conditions.

Beef cattle are less prominent. Quebec raises only 20 per cent of what it requires, and much of the herd is located in the Abitibi region and the Ottawa valley. In these areas beef cattle — particularly Herefords — outnumber dairy cows. Elsewhere, the government has encouraged farmers to slaughter surplus dairy cows.

In poultry operations, Quebec produces 25 per cent more broiler chickens than it consumes, and has the capacity to produce even more. However, too few turkeys are produced to satisfy the demand, and birds must be brought in from outside the province. Eggs must also be imported, for Quebec produces only 55 per cent of its requirements.

IN THE FIELDS

Crop production contributes only 10 per cent of total agricultural income in Quebec. A major share of its significance is hidden, as livestock producers grow forage and grain crops to feed their animals, and these crops are consumed rather than sold.

Of these crops the most important are forage varieties. The average Quebec farm grows 20 ha of alfalfa or lucerne and a further 13 ha of pasture, aiming to produce winter and summer feed respectively. However, the Quebec government has encouraged farmers to use their land for crops which produce higher returns.

The second most abundant field crop after alfalfa is corn, which is produced both as silage feed and as grain feed. Silage corn can be produced in most regions of the province, but corn for grain feed takes longer to mature and needs more 'thermal units' — the heat required to enable it to grow, which is adequate only in southern parts of the province. Many dairy producers in counties of the Ste. Hyacinthe region grow their own corn grain to be used as grain feed. Those elsewhere in Quebec grow alternative grain crops, notably oats. Otherwise they rely on mixes of corn, oats, and barley brought from western Canada.

Other field crops important in Quebec include potatoes and industrial produce like tobacco and sugar beets, which require processing before use. Potatoes need slightly acidic, light, sandy loam and are grown on specialist farms in the east of the province, north of Montreal, and in the region of Quebec City. Tobacco requires sandy soil with little organic matter, of the sort that is found in Joliette, north of Montreal, and in the Richelieu valley. Both pipe tobacco (dried naturally) and cigarette tobacco (dried in kilns) are produced, and nearly 800 growers are involved.

Sugar beet production is concentrated in three counties of the Ste. Hyacinthe region, close to the government-operated sugar refinery in St. Hilaire, which processes the crop. Sugar beets thrive in well-drained, stoneless, deep, clay loam. There have been efforts to introduce oilseed crops like soybeans and rapeseed, but appropriate refineries have not been built.

Fruit and vegetable production is important on Montreal island and in counties to the south, which have suitable climate and rich organic soil. The fresh food markets of Montreal and its region are close at hand, and so are the plants of canned and frozen food processors.

Carrots and corn make up nearly half the value of production for the fresh vegetable market, while other varieties commonly produced include cabbages, lettuce, tomatoes, onions, cucumbers, and a dozen more. Peas, beans, and sweet corn for processing are grown on

A Quebec farmer applies anhydrous ammonia fertilizer to a field of corn.

![Hay farming scene with tractors]

Hay (including alfalfa) is Quebec's most abundant crop. In most cases it is grown in association with dairy farming operations. This is a farm in the region of Plessisville, in south-eastern Quebec.

farms operated by the processors or by local farmers under contract.

Apples and strawberries are the major features of fruit production in the province. Apples — particularly the McIntosh — are grown in hilly regions like Rouville and neighbouring counties south-east of Montreal, where the sub-soil is drained well enough to ensure that tree roots are not drowned.

Rising labour costs force all crop farmers to consider improved mechanization, but that costs money too, and many farmers under-utilize their land's potential in spite of generous government subsidies. An ominous example of their difficulties is the rising proportion of the apple crop processed as cider, for which the picking date is less relevant, rather than as fresh fruit, which must be picked at precisely the right state of ripeness and thus needs extra labour for harvesting.

Potatoes are a specialty crop in the east of the province and near Montreal and Quebec City. They thrive in slightly acidic, light, sandy soil.

Pipe and cigarette tobacco is produced in Joliette, north of Montreal, and in the Richelieu valley. Here picked leaves are transported to the kilns in which they will be dried.

Northern Quebec has millions of kilometres of boreal pulpwood forest, as yet undeveloped. Forests are Canada's most valuable renewable resource, though in Quebec's case they are rivalled by abundant hydro-electric potential.

TREES AND FORESTS

Agricultural land in Quebec was developed from cleared forests, and in many areas farmers still derive an appreciable income from original timber stands. Others plant seedling trees on cleared land not suitable for profitable farming.

Many types of seedling are available for planting; they vary according to terrain, soil, and climate. In the Eastern Townships, which are in any case heavily wooded, many farmers develop plantations of 'Christmas trees' — balsam fir or Scotch pine regularly pruned to develop a distinctive conical shape.

Also in the Eastern Townships and indeed right through Southern Quebec, many farmers gain further income from stands of maple trees from which they tap sugar sap each spring. The maple sugar industry is one of the oldest in North America, adopted by early white settlers from local Indians.

All maple species produce a sap of some kind, but the sugar maple yields most syrup per litre of sap. The ideal tree for sap production has a short bole, topped with abundant foliage. A hole is bored into the trunk, sloping upwards to allow the sap to flow down. A spout is inserted into the hole. In one system commonly used, the spout is connected to a plastic pipe, which leads to a network of such pipes draining into a tank. The sap should be collected within forty-eight hours of being tapped, and must be filtered and then boiled as soon as possible.

The tapping season begins in mid-March and continues well into April, until the weather becomes too warm. Some producers sponsor commercial sugaring-off parties for visitors, featuring favourite syrup recipes, but 90 per cent of production is channeled to marketing firms. Quebec accounts for about 75 per

cent of Canada's production, and most of it is exported to the United States.

The Quebec maple forest is divided into three zones. The hickory-maple zone centres on Montreal and occupies all the south-western corner of the province on the St. Lawrence. The sugar maple predominates, along with other deciduous hardwoods like the hickory, hornbeam, and elm. All are of great commercial value in the lumber industry.

Surrounding this zone and extending to a point just beyond Quebec City is the laurentian maple zone, in which sugar maples amount to 30 per cent of the trees and other hardwoods are present too.

The yellow birch-maple zone covers most of the Eastern Townships, the Saguenay river valley, and much of the Ottawa valley. This third zone is essentially a mixed-wood forest, containing

A feature of maple-syrup production is the 'sugaring-off' party, in which boiling syrup is poured onto fresh snow, where it congeals. This is a scene at a sugar lodge at St. Raphael in Bellechasse, south of the St. Lawrence near the Ile d'Orléans.

both hardwoods and softwoods — the hardwoods being sugar maple, yellow birch, and beech. It was this zone which provided the great white pines, the softwood conifers which were the basis of Quebec's lumber industry throughout the nineteenth century.

Earlier, cargoes of oak had been carried to France for shipbuilding, and in the seigneuries, all the oaks and minerals had been reserved for the king. But it was pine that had led lumberjacks into the interior, particularly after the British turned to the Canadian forests in 1808 during the Napoleonic wars.

The initial demand was for 'squared' timber shaped on the spot, and later for 'deal' timber (large planks) cut in Canadian sawmills. At first the British government encouraged entrepreneurs to develop Canadian resources, but during the nineteenth century their tariff protection steadily diminished.

In any case, the pine industry exhausted itself as lumberjacks moved farther into the interior, and it became steadily less economic to exploit what remained. Instead, modest local sawmills were built to exploit other species. Later came the great pulp and paper industry, which concentrated on the smaller coniferous softwoods of the Gaspé Peninsula and the north. These softwoods make up by far the bulk of Quebec's commercial forest. The latter extends in two bands across the province: one, the fir zone in the south, a transition area between the deciduous and coniferous forests; the other the spruce zone of spruce and fir, reaching to the shores of James Bay.

Even power saws are being made redundant by the introduction of mechanical harvesters. These grip a tree, sheer its limbs, top it, snip the bottom of its trunk, and stack it as a log, all in one swift operation.

Harvesting the forest has always been hard work, and modern lumberjacks eat as heartily as their forebears.

31

Canadair CL-215 water-bombers were specially designed to fight fires and were introduced in 1967. The Quebec government has a fleet of fifteen of these aircraft, which are stationed at points throughout the forest regions.

The CL-215 scoops water from a lake or river, then 'bombs' its target before returning to scoop another load. The aircraft is an amphibian, and can be used in aerial spraying and air patrol, in resource surveying, and as heavy transport.

CONSERVATION

Forests are among Quebec's most valuable assets. They are threatened by pests and disease, but the provincial government takes steps to eradicate these menaces. Much more serious is the danger of wildfire, the most spectacular of natural disasters.

On average, there are more than 1000 outbreaks of wildfire in Quebec each year. Some are caused by lightning, but eight out of ten start through carelessness, particularly of campers and hunters. Apart from the waste involved, wildfire may have serious consequences for the whole environment for decades to come.

True, a degree of wildfire is natural in the forest and is to some extent even necessary. Some species — notably the jack pine — cannot reproduce without it, as heat is required to open their cones. Also, fire may help to clear dead and mature trees to make way for thrusting saplings, which require strong sunlight to develop.

Wildfire in mature green forests leaves many of the trees still alive. Far worse are fires in areas piled high in dried timber 'slash,' the residue of timber cutting operations. In such cases the topsoil is burned, and with it the seeds that would have produced new growth.

Care of the forests is a provincial concern. Quebec's policy has been to make forest concession-holders responsible for preventing and controlling fires in their areas. In former days, when most forest work was done in winter, fire protection provided handy summer employment for forest workers otherwise idle. In recent decades, however, patterns in the industry have changed. Higher labour costs have encouraged companies to turn to mechanization, and improved techniques (particularly in transportation) mean that forestry now takes place chiefly in summer. The worst period of the fire season is early summer, when many hundreds of fires break out. Few men are available for fire watches, so the industry has turned to aerial patrols.

Since 1972 fire protection and control in Quebec has been in the hands of seven incorporated *sociétés de conservation* approved by the province. Each is responsible for a particular area, and between them they cover all of the commercial forest. Membership consists of concession-holders in each area and also the provincial government. Each *société* must carry out fire patrols in its area at members' expense, but half the actual cost of fighting fires is borne by the province. The valuable forests of the south are given intensive protection, marginal forests in the middle have limited protection, but the relatively barren north has none.

The *sociétés* have their own patrol aircraft and they also contract with private pilots flying their own aircraft. However, for fire-fighting they draw on the province's fleet of water-bombers — Canadair CL-215s, specially designed for the job, and veteran Cansos introduced in World War II. These aircraft are on stand-by throughout the fire season. The Canadair CL-215 is capable of extinguishing a normal forest fire unaided, bombing it with a blanket of water scooped up from a nearby lake or river. In more serious outbreaks two or more aircraft may be used.

Fire-fighting techniques utilizing the CL-215s have become very sophisticated. But as yet no antidote has been found for the dreaded 'crown fire' — one that spreads through the crowns of coniferous trees during a high wind. In such circumstances ground crews must be trucked in or flown in by helicopter to create an emergency firebreak, a belt of land cleared of trees.

The *sociétés* may introduce deterrents to pests and disease at their discretion and at the expense of the provincial government, provided it has authorized the scheme. This has been important in the Gaspé Peninsula, which has been plagued by the spread of the spruce budworm.

Fur Trapping

Quebec's early prosperity rested on the fur trade — as much from the hinterland north of the St. Lawrence and the Gulf as from the lands in the west where Montreal's North West Company battled England's Hudson's Bay Company until the rival parties came to terms and amalgamated in 1821.

North of the St. Lawrence there was originally keen rivalry between French traders and the Hudson's Bay Company. The French built trading posts north of Lac St. Jean, to combat the influence of English posts on James Bay. Actual trapping was left to Indians, who transported pelts by canoe to the trading post of their fancy.

As happened elsewhere in Canada, exploitation of the beaver in Quebec during the 1920s and 1930s was so great that the species faced extinction, and from 1932 a series of beaver reserves was set aside. When the beaver regained its former strength, trapping by Indians was resumed, but this time it was closely supervised.

Today Quebec produces about 25 per cent of the total value of Canada's annual beaver catch, and about one-sixth of the value of all pelts produced — notably muskrat, red fox, lynx, raccoon, white fox, and (in the north on a Hudson Bay) hair seal, caught by Inuit. There are also many mink farms in Western Quebec. Much of the province's annual pelt production is forwarded to fur processors and manufacturers in Montreal.

The beaver, *Castor canadensis*

PULP AND PAPER

Three-quarters of Quebec's commercial forest consists of softwoods suited to pulp and paper production. The remaining quarter is hardwood, normally processed as lumber or veneer. In practice there is considerable overlap.

More than nine-tenths of the total forest area is publicly owned, administered by the provincial government, and in most instances leased to pulp and paper manufacturers or lumber mills. However, the privately owned forests are closer to markets and provide disproportionate quantities of both pulpwood and lumber.

In the past, publicly owned forests were leased virtually in perpetuity, though producers had to take out annual cutting licences, which could be withheld if they failed to respect forest legislation. In particular they were expected to file detailed inventories and management plans, which they were required to observe.

In 1972, however, the province introduced a ten-year plan to phase out the old system and, instead, rationalize timber limits. This means that each established forest industry is allocated adequate timber resources to provide its raw materials, which are drawn from relatively larger tracts, making possible controlled and efficient management.

The province's timber industry is lucrative and supports more than five hundred sawmills, but the pulp and paper industry is much larger. Quebec produces more than one-third of Canada's pulp and paper total, and in newsprint produces more than half of Canada's total and 20 per cent of the world's. In all there are nearly sixty plants in the province involved in pulp and paper making, though some produce only pulp and others only paper. The biggest are integrated plants, which undertake all processes from grinding logs to rolling newsprint. The process can be described simply, but it involves sophisticated chemistry.

Logs cut in the forest are debarked at the plant, then forwarded to either of two main processes used to produce pulp — groundwood and chemical. Groundwood pulp is produced when the logs are pressed against whirling grindstones or rotating discs, which tear at the wood and shred the fibres (cells) of which it is composed.

In the chemical process, logs are first reduced to wood chips. These are screened and tipped into a 'digester,' where they are cooked under pressure in chemical liquors which dissolve the lignin that binds fibres to their neighbours. According to the chemicals used, the pulp produced may be sulphate (kraft) or sulphite. Each of these has special qualities, particularly of strength and stability.

Quality woodpulp papers are made almost exclusively from chemical pulp (though the finest papers of all are hand-made from cotton pulp, the purest cellulose). Newsprint is relatively coarse, and about 80 per cent of its content is groundwood pulp.

Once the groundwood and chemical pulp have been mixed in appropriate proportions, and perhaps treated with bleach or dye or other chemicals to provide special properties, they are forwarded to the paper mill. The basic principle of paper making is that individual wet fibres adhere to each other as they are dried. The pulp is heavily diluted with water. The mixture flows on to a moving wire mesh screen, the 'foudrinier.' Most of the water drains through this screen, and by the time the pulp reaches the end of the foudrinier, it is strong enough to support its own weight. At this point it is transferred to a heavy felt blanket.

It reaches a series of press rolls which wring out still more water, then passes over a series of steam-heated cylinders which dry it. Finally the sheet winds down a series of calender rolls, which iron it and produce a smooth finish. The whole process, start to finish, may take no more than ten seconds.

Nearly all the paper made in Canada is produced on foudrinier machines. But paperboard is usually made on cylinder machines, where sheets are formed from several layers of pulp. Felt on these machines collects these layers from cylinders revolving in separate vats of pulp, and carries the assembled sheet to rollers and dryers.

Sawmills are sited in the hardwood and mixed forests of Southern Quebec. This one is at Marsoui in the Gaspé, where lumber is a major industry.

Fall colours highlight a large pulp and paper mill at Shawinigan on the St. Maurice river. A pyramid of logs awaits processing in the plant.

Rolls of newsprint are the end product of complex processes at the Grand'Mère pulp and paper mill, located on the St. Maurice river. Grand'Mère is so named because of a distinctive rock formation resembling an old woman's face.

Gaspésienne fishing smacks trail long lines to catch cod. Each line carries 2 m casts, from which dangle baited hooks.

In some villages cod is salted and dried in the sun, ready for export to European markets.

FISHING FLEETS

Quebec's fishing industry is tiny compared with the provincial economy as a whole. But in eastern Gaspé and the Magdalen Islands, and along the north shore of the St. Lawrence, it is an essential mainstay of the regional economy.

The rich fishing grounds of Canada's Atlantic coast were being exploited by French and Basque fishing fleets before Jacques Cartier's first expedition in 1534. Those early fishermen concentrated on cod. They 'dry-salted' much of it ashore, gutting and cleaning the fish and spreading them on wooden racks or 'flakes' to dry in the sun.

The Basques dropped out of the picture, and in the eighteenth century the English and New Englanders forced the French to fall back on the St. Lawrence shore, the Gaspé Peninsula, and Cape Breton Island. Some of their modern successors continue to sun-dry their catch for European markets, which favour the salted product.

Groundfish (those feeding on the bottom), like cod and redfish, are still an important part of Quebec's annual catch. The fish are caught by hand-line from small boats relatively close to shore, from longliners (notably Gaspésienne smacks) which trail lines bearing 2 m casts on which dangle hooks, and from trawlers which drag bag-like nets through the water.

Today, most of the catch is filleted, then chilled or frozen for the North American market. The advantages of pre-filleting are reduction of weight (an important factor in transportation) and easier cooking at home. Offal (waste) from the filleting may be processed for use in fertilizers, fish meal, vitamins, and industrial oils.

However, groundfish have been increasingly scarce in recent years, because of over-exploitation far out to sea by international fishing fleets, and some over-fishing in the home fishery too. Other species of edible finfish have also been depleted. These include herring (which swim in schools and are caught by purse-seining — surrounding the shoal with a net) and the once-abundant Atlantic salmon.

Recently there has been more emphasis on the lobster and shrimp fishery,

with an eye to lucrative export markets in the United States. The lobsters are caught in traps by relatively small craft not far off-shore. Once landed they are in most cases canned or frozen.

There is an annual seal hunt in Quebec, not as extensive as those off Newfoundland and Labrador. There is a significant eel fishery in the St. Lawrence, and in addition a growing freshwater fishery up the river and inland, which has provided a useful sideline for local farmers.

Herring is one of the species caught in the Gulf of St. Lawrence.

The most famous fishing village in the Gaspé is Percé, at the eastern tip of the peninsula. It is named after Percé (pierced) rock, a limestone formation in which the sea has tunnelled a spectacular arch.

The Gaspé

Perhaps the most picturesque region of Quebec is Gaspésie, the Gaspé Peninsula on the south side of the Gulf of St. Lawrence. It is part of the Appalachian system, and its interior contains the charmingly named Shickshock mountains, which include the highest peaks in Eastern Canada.

Subsistence fishing was long the chief economic activity of this region, for there is little arable land for farming, and much of what there is has not been accessible. In this century, however, forestry has developed as a major industry, and there is important revenue, too, from activities associated with the rich Gaspé copper mine.

The Gaspé's greatest potential is tourism. It remains a region little spoiled and full of charm and interest. Most visitors make a beeline for Percé, the great pierced rock at the peninsula's eastern tip. But there is much more to be discovered than Percé alone, both along the coast and in the interior.

ASBESTOS

The term asbestos originally meant 'unquenchable,' referring to a legendary stone which once set ablaze could never be put out. In its modern sense, however, asbestos cannot catch fire in the first place.

Actually, asbestos is a whole family of fibrous, silicate minerals with a bewildering range of qualities. It includes amosite and crocidolite, but the most significant is chrysotile, which accounts for 95 per cent of world consumption of asbestos. Canada produces 40 per cent of the world's chrysotile, 80 per cent of it from Quebec.

The first asbestos mine in Quebec was opened in 1878, in the Thetford region of the Eastern Townships. Since then a number of mines have been developed along a 100 km belt in the region, extending east from the town of Asbestos, the site of the world's largest known deposit.

Chrysotile fibres are made up of sheets of atoms curled up like rolls of carpet. It is supposed that they resulted from molten silica from the earth's magma circulating in fissures in igneous rock and eventually recrystallizing in their present form. In colour they range from olive green to greenish-white.

Though some asbestos is mined underground, the typical asbestos operation is an open pit — a hole progressively deepened or extended as the lay of the ore body dictates. To minimize collapses, the sides of the pit are stepped back in 10 m 'benches,' which make the mine look like an amphitheatre.

After drilling, blasting, and sorting, the ore is trucked to crushers which break up the rock. At this stage it is comparatively wet, so it must be dried — in vertical towers if the material is fine, and in horizontal driers if it is coarse. Next it passes over vibrating screens, which filter out the finer particles.

Coarser materials are crushed smaller. They are passed over shaking

The open pit asbestos mine at Black Rock, Eastern Townships, is stepped back to prevent cave-ins. In the distance are processing plants.

screens, which leave the asbestos fibres 'floating' on top. The fibres are sucked off by 'aspiration' and are conveyed to fibre collectors, while the remaining ore goes on for further crushing. The process is repeated until all fibres have been recovered.

Fibre recovered by this process is cleaned by repeated screening, and separated into commercial grades according to length and quality. Quebec producers classify their products in eight main categories, though there are several hundred variations. The product is packaged for the market.

Production from the asbestos belt of the Eastern Townships has reached a plateau, though at current rates it should continue for several more decades. Elsewhere in the province other rich deposits are being developed, notably in the Abitibi region of the west and at Cape Ungava in the far north, where a mine was opened in 1972.

One criticism of Quebec's asbestos industry is that nearly all its production is exported in the raw state, without any effort made to process it further. It could be that a much larger secondary processing industry will develop, particularly in the spinning of asbestos cloth and in the manufacturing of products that use asbestos fibres as binding agents. The industry has also been attacked for the health hazards that asbestos fibres pose. There is evidence that in sufficient quantities they can damage lungs, make breathing difficult, and eventually promote cancer. Regulations have been introduced to minimize fibrous dust concentrate in mills and factories.

Following blasting, asbestos ore is loaded into heavy trucks for conveyance to crushers. This is a scene at Black Rock mine in the Eastern Townships' asbestos belt.

Thetford Mines in the Eastern Townships was the location of Quebec's first asbestos mine, opened in 1878. Since then mines have been developed along a 100 km belt.

Trade Unions

A four-month strike at Asbestos in 1949 was punctuated by skirmishes between strikers and police. There had been industry-wide strikes in Quebec before, but none so well-publicized, and the conflict helped Quebeckers working in industry to understand the value of their labour and its use as a bargaining tool.

Trade unionism in Quebec had its roots in the nineteenth century. But with encouragement from bishops in small dioceses, unions (*syndicats*) founded after 1900 were usually confessional (Roman Catholic), and were 'national' in that they catered to French Canadians across Canada. The church's influence in these unions was often considerable. The *Confédération des Travailleurs Catholiques du Canada*, formed after World War I, helped consolidate this position. Quebec unions were very different from the predominantly socialist 'Red Flag' unions elsewhere. Out of touch with 'international' unions, they were sometimes accused of undermining the labour movement and selling labour too cheaply.

Following World War II, Quebec unions became more left-wing and the church's influence diminished — to the disgust of Maurice Duplessis, who maintained that Quebeckers had no place in industry. But the Lesage administration invited several top labour leaders to take up positions with the government. They were replaced in the unions by younger men, who moved even further left to keep in tune with the times.

METALS

Traditionally, Quebec's major strengths in metals mining have been copper and zinc. However, major new iron ore deposits are being developed along the Labrador trench and elsewhere, and Quebec is likely to become Canada's largest iron ore producer.

The first metals mine worked in Quebec was a lead deposit opened on the instigation of the intendant Jean Talon, near Little Gaspé on the north shore of Gaspé Bay. The miners' tunnel may still be seen on the shoreline, though it is now almost completely flooded at high tide.

Earlier, Jacques Cartier persistently searched for the source of copper he had found in the hands of St. Lawrence Indians — not realizing that a rich deposit lay within Gaspésie. But near Stadacona he did discover what he believed to be gold and diamonds, and took them to Europe as proof of the new land's great wealth. Unfortunately the gold was pyrite and the diamonds were mica. The French at home were disgusted, and some still speak of anything worthless as 'a Canadian diamond.' Only the increasing prospects of the fur trade encouraged them to look again at Canada.

In the later 1600s iron ore was found near Trois Rivières, and from the 1730s it was processed in local works. Following the Cariboo gold rush of the 1860s in British Columbia, there was a spate of prospecting for placer gold, and modest success in the 1930s prefaced the opening of small gold mines in Val d'Or in the Abitibi region.

The first true base-metals mine was established at St. Eustis in the Eastern Townships, a copper deposit which continued production until World War II. In 1910 a small lead-zinc mine opened in Portneuf county, on the St. Lawrence river near Quebec City. At this time, too, Noranda was discovered east of Lake Abitibi.

Noranda, part of an enormous field of copper, is just across the border from the rich precious metal deposits discovered in Northern Ontario soon after the start of the century. At the time the area swarmed with prospectors, and the Noranda deposit was located in 1911

The great Gaspé copper mine of Murdochville is a major influence on the region's economy.

by Ed Horne, who had been looking for gold and silver.

The Noranda mine and the nearby gold-mining camp, Rouyn, came into

At underground copper and zinc mines in the Noranda region, miners drill the hanging wall (ceiling) to insert roofbolts, a safety measure designed to prevent rockfalls.

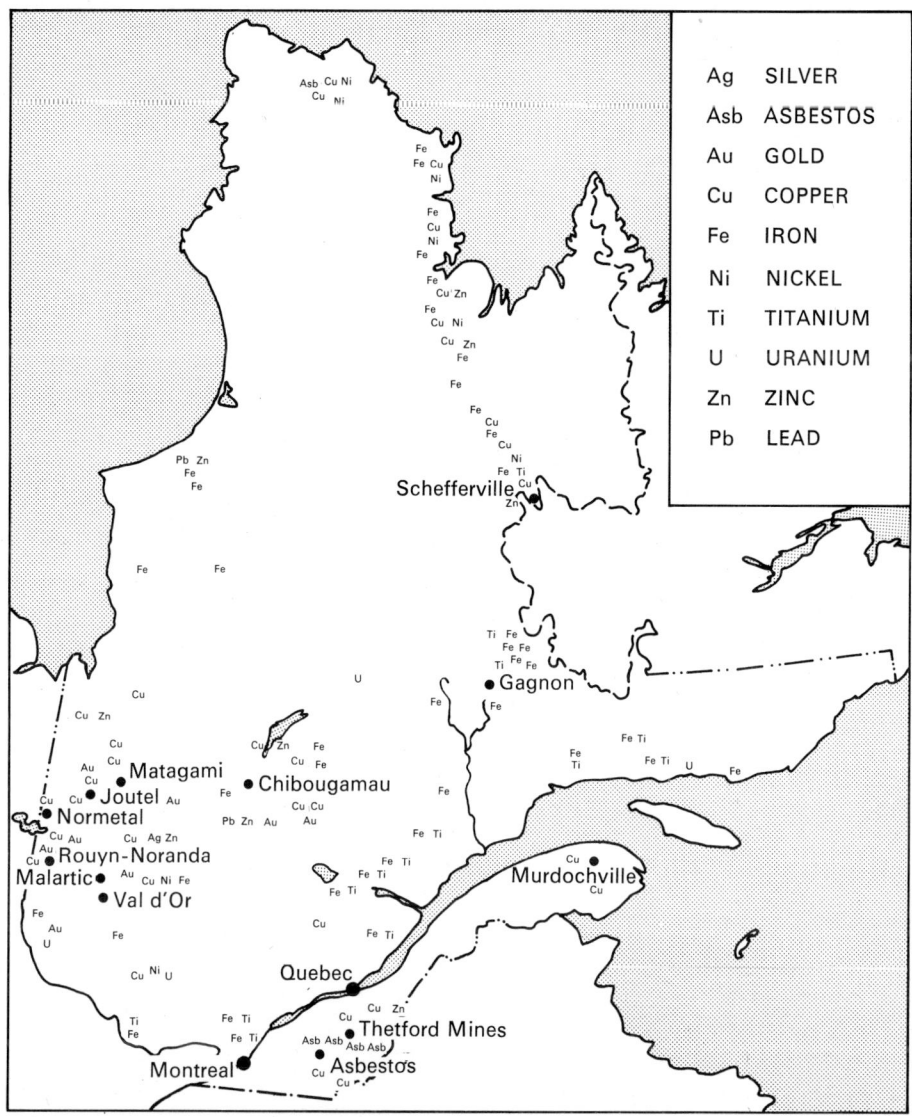

Ag	SILVER
Asb	ASBESTOS
Au	GOLD
Cu	COPPER
Fe	IRON
Ni	NICKEL
Ti	TITANIUM
U	URANIUM
Zn	ZINC
Pb	LEAD

Copper, asbestos, and immense reserves of iron ore in Northern Quebec are the province's most valued mineral resources.

The Mount Wright iron ore mine on the Labrador trench is being sunk to a point 300 m below ground level. Nearby are crushers and concentrators, which process the ore before it is transported to Port Cartier on the Gulf of St. Lawrence.

At Schefferville, iron ore is blasted and then loaded into heavy trucks by a mechanical shovel, to be transported to crushers and concentrators.

being in the 1920s. At the time, the four Murray brothers of the Gaspé Peninsula were exploring a 'copper mountain' that they had discovered there. But their mine did not come into production until 1951, by which time other mines in the Abitibi area were already established.

Deposits in the Noranda–Rouyn area are nearing exhaustion, though others have been developed farther north around Matagami and Chibougamau. They are worked both as open pits and by underground methods, as is the Gaspé mine.

The iron ore mines of the Labrador trench are worked as open pits. Iron ore blasted from these mines is crushed nearby, and may be transported to the coast in that form to be exported or may be 'beneficiated.' This involves first grinding the ore, then spinning a slurry of ore and water in a series of spirals, which separate out heavy metal particles by specific gravity.

Tailings (wastes) from the spirals are fed through a magnetic separator, which picks out any remaining magnetic particles. The finished concentrate is reground, then fed into a balling drum along with bentonite to act as a binder. The balling drum rolls wet 'pellets' of iron ore, which are then dried.

Finished pellets are shipped to steel mills in Canada and elsewhere, particularly to those in Hamilton. The elimination of so much waste rock means that less energy will be required to smelt pig iron from the ore, so that the eventual cost of steel production should be appreciably lower.

Other metals are produced in Quebec, particularly a group used as additives to steel because of special qualities they contribute. These include columbium deposits developed near Montreal and near Chicoutimi in the Saguenay valley. Besides, Quebec is Canada's only producer of titanium dioxide. The deposit of titanium at Allard Lake, about 40 km inland from the Gulf of St. Lawrence, is the largest in the world yet discovered. The ore is shipped to Sorel, near Montreal, for beneficiation, and is processed as the major raw material for the production of titanium dioxide pigments for use in paint.

The Noranda copper refinery in Montreal is the world's largest. It handles copper from mines all over Eastern Canada. Behind it is one of the oil refineries that are the basis of Quebec's petrochemical manufacturing industry.

SMELTERS AND REFINERIES

Much of Quebec's mineral potential has still to be explored, and actual output of mineral ore has been modest compared with Ontario's and British Columbia's. On the other hand, Quebec is a world leader in the refining industry.

The first significant metal smelting and refining operations were introduced following the opening of the Noranda copper mines in the 1920s. A smelter was built at Noranda and has been steadily enlarged, until today it is the world's largest custom copper smelter. The original Noranda copper deposits are nearly exhausted, and the smelter now processes ore from other mines both within Quebec and outside.

Noranda's giant electrolytic copper refinery in Montreal East, established in 1931, handles copper from mines in provinces from Newfoundland to Saskatchewan. It is responsible for more than half of Canada's total production of refined copper, and is the biggest copper refinery in the world.

Various by-products are recovered as a result of the refining process. Among them are silver, and the Montreal refinery is Canada's largest single source of refined silver. About one-third of the copper produced goes to Canadian manufacturers, and the rest is exported.

At Valleyfield, north on the St. Lawrence from Montreal, is the copper refinery's twin, the electrolytic zinc re-

finery, where production began in 1973. It is owned by five mining companies operating in Quebec or across the border in north-east Ontario. The refinery processes concentrate first roasted in a chemical plant.

Before 1972, Quebec's steel industry was modest, relying on scrap metal as its raw material. However, the development of important iron ore mines in the north-eastern interior has encouraged the emergence of an integrated steel industry, which can be expanded if new markets can be developed.

Iron ore for the Quebec steelworks is mined at Fire Lake, north of the Gulf of St. Lawrence, then railed to Port Cartier, where it is pelletized. Half the production is shipped to the Sidbec–Dosco plant at Contrecoeur, between Montreal and Quebec City on the south bank of the St. Lawrence. Here flat-rolled steel, rods, and bars are produced.

Considering the immense supplies of raw materials available, Quebec has been slow to develop a steel industry. However, the omission is offset by remarkable achievements in handling a mineral foreign to Canada — bauxite, the chief source of aluminum. The province has four fully integrated aluminum smelters. The first of these was completed in 1901 at Shawinigan on the St. Maurice river, utilizing the abundant hydroelectricity available. Before long, demand in Canada outstripped supply, and the company turned to the Saguenay river, just below Lac St. Jean, where immense power could be harnessed.

The Saguenay development at Arvida came into production in 1926, drawing its raw materials from a new source — British Guiana (Guyana since 1970) in South America. The British government insisted that Guianan bauxite should be processed within the British Empire, and Canadians prepared to compete with American production. By 1945, thanks to the hydroelectricity available, the Arvida plant was the world's largest, and with subsequent expansions it has remained so. Other smelters are in operation at Beauharnois near Montreal (operated by Alcan Canada like those at Arvida and Shawinigan) and at Cap de la Madeleine near Trois Rivières.

Before reaching these smelters, bauxite from the suppliers is treated with hot caustic soda, which dissolves the alumina hydrate it contains and leaves behind 'red mud' (aluminum oxide). At the smelter the 'red mud' is dissolved in cryolite in the heated 'pot.' A powerful electric current is passed through the solution. The current separates the 'mud' into aluminum metal and oxygen gas. The gas combines with carbon and bubbles off as carbon dioxide, while the molten metal sinks to the bottom and is siphoned into large crucibles. Other metals may be added to make aluminum alloys, and the alloys are then cast.

Bars of copper are poured at the custom copper smelter, Noranda, in Abitibi. The copper is sent to Montreal for refining.

In the aluminum smelter, electrically produced heat is applied to aluminum oxide ('red mud') and a chemical reaction separates molten aluminum from the oxygen which accompanies it. Here a potman breaks the crust formed from molten aluminum pouring from a cell.

The emergence of integrated steelworks adds stature to heavy industry in Quebec. This is the Sidbec–Dosco plant at Contrecoeur on the St. Lawrence, between Montreal and Quebec City.

The snowmobile is a Quebec invention. Here machines are assembled in a plant near Montreal.

MANUFACTURING

In 1668 the intendant Jean Talon applied to the French king for permission to develop iron ore deposits discovered near Trois Rivières, hoping to set up an ironworks and produce iron implements and perhaps armaments. Permission was refused.

At the time, France (like England) regarded colonies as captive markets for exports, and blocked efforts to establish home industry. Talon was allowed to found a brewery (the Brasserie du Roi in Quebec City in 1671) and shipyards (also in Quebec), but the Trois Rivières ironworks was not approved until 1738.

The effort produced the finest industrial achievement of the French regime. A metal-forger from New France visited New England to observe smelting techniques employed there, and by 1741 his furnaces were supplying all Quebec with such items as cooking pots, heating stoves, axes, and hammers. Les Forges Saint-Maurice was soon the biggest ironworks in North America, and produced the armaments used by New France against England in the Seven Years' War.

The technology developed made it possible for a Montreal firm to produce most of the complex engine castings required for Canada's first steamboat, the *Accommodation*. This early effort was a paddle-wheeler launched near Montreal in 1809. Subsequent years saw a succession of such vessels, designed for use on the St. Lawrence between Montreal and Quebec City. In 1833 the *Royal William* (hull built in Quebec City and engine in Montreal) was the first ship to cross the Atlantic on steam alone.

By now Montreal was Canada's chief manufacturing centre, and it received a great boost during the American civil war of the 1860s, when for the first time Canadian manufacturers had their domestic market to themselves. The need to protect it was a major factor in bringing about Confederation.

In subsequent years Quebec continued to concentrate on consumer products distributed throughout Eastern Canada by the transport routes emanating from Montreal. Meanwhile Ontario was laying the basis of its heavier machine-tool industry, which at first complemented Quebec production, but during the two world wars overshadowed it.

In general terms the difference remains — to Quebec's disadvantage. Its light production can be matched in other countries, where labour costs are far lower. These countries can land products in Canada far more cheaply in spite of tariff hedges. As a result, the relative importance of consumer industries — foods and beverages, tobacco products, rubber, leather, textiles, knitted goods, and clothing — has dropped. They now account for less than 40 per cent of employment in the manufacturing sector, and less than 35 per cent of value added per man-hour.

A second group of industries is related to the processing of forest products — wood, furniture and fixtures, paper and allied products, and printing and publishing. This group has gained overall, though its chief element (paper and allied products) has declined. In employment it accounts for more than 20 per cent, in value added for 22 per cent.

A third group consists of metallurgical products, technically within the manufacturing sectors though often considered primary. Owing largely to increased steel and aluminum production, it accounts for about 12 per cent of manufacturing employment and nearly 15 per cent of value added.

The fourth group is composed chiefly of equipment goods and durable goods — machinery, transportation equipment, and electrical products — and upon them depends Quebec's manufacturing future. Their share of value added has risen to nearly 15 per cent, and employment has reached more than 15 per cent.

Quebec is a world leader in manufacturing electronics (notably telecommunications) equipment. In transportation the province's shipyards and aviation manufacturers have experienced unsettling fluctuations, but the Quebec-invented snowmobile has been an international success.

The final manufacturing group — non-metallic mineral products, petroleum and coal products, and chemicals — is related chiefly to subsequent manufacturers rather than to the con-

'Billets' are cast continously, six at a time, at the Contrecoeur steelworks.

sumer sector, though part of the petroleum and chemical output reaches it. Its share of value added stands at about 13 per cent, while employment is less than 10 per cent.

Quebec City's first shipyard was established by intendant Jean Talon in the seventeenth century. The tradition continues across the St. Lawrence at Lauzon, near Lévis.

Distribution

Greater Montreal remains Quebec's industrial focus, and 70 per cent of Quebec's manufacturing activity is concentrated in the Montreal agglomeration. For some industries the concentration is even higher — 97 per cent for petroleum products, 88 per cent for knitted goods, and 87 per cent for electrical products.

Five other regions contribute substantial shares of overall production, through geographic location and the availability of specific production factors such as labour and cheap power. Most important after Montreal is Quebec City, which produces food and beverages, leather, tobacco, paper, knitted goods, and ships.

The Trois Rivières–Shawinigan region produces wood, paper, and textiles. The Eastern Townships — especially Sherbrooke and Drummondville — produce textiles, clothing, paper, food, and beverages. The Saguenay–Lac St. Jean region produces aluminum and paper. Hull is an important centre of pulp and paper production.

A problem throughout the province has been low industrial productivity compared with current levels in Canada as a whole, and Ontario in particular. This has been the result of soaring wage costs in the light consumer goods sector, where these represent a high proportion (32 per cent in clothing) of total production expense.

TEXTILES AND CLOTHING

The categories in which manufacturing industries are classified give no hint of the complex links that bind them. A finished product may involve contributions from a dozen or more separate factories, acting independently or in succession.

An example is the world of textiles and clothing, the manufacturing industries most closely identified with Quebec, and particularly with Montreal and the Eastern Townships. Their operations commence with the raw material — natural fibres like wool and cotton, or man-made filaments like polyester, nylon, and dacron.

Polyester yarn, for example, is the result of a series of complex processes which convert petrochemical feedstock, drawn from an oil refinery, into polymer flakes. These are melted at high temperature, and the mixture is 'extruded' under pressure through tiny holes. The continuous filament that results is quickly dried and twisted with other filaments to form yarn, which is, at this stage, white. Other processes are used to give the raw yarn particular qualities, and it may be forwarded to a dying house. Then it will be despatched to a textile mill to be knitted or woven.

Similarly complex processes govern the manufacture of wool and cotton yarn, which may each contain elements of man-made fibres to give them added advantages. Both wool and cotton are first cleaned, then carded on tiny needles which comb the fluffy fibres into line ready for spinning into yarn.

The long-time distinction between knitting and weaving has been blurred with the introduction of a wide range of sophisticated machine processes. Basically weaving involves two sets of yarn, the warp lengthways and the weft crossways. Knitting involves only one, and successive rows are interstitched.

Some textile mills produce finished consumer articles — for instance, blankets, bedspreads, drapes, and carpets. Each involves a number of processes, and a mill usually specializes in one family of products which may then be forwarded for finishing. Again, some mills specialize in industrial products, for instance nylon tire core.

Teams of seam-stitchers with sewing machines assemble components into garments in a Montreal clothing factory.

A few mills are actually apparel manufacturers, for instance, hosiery mills which make socks and stockings, and clothing factories which knit 'fully fashioned' (designed to a pattern) components of outerwear, like pullovers. But other mills produce cloth to supply the garment industry proper.

Mills rely heavily on machinery, and are therefore chiefly capital-intensive. In contrast, clothing factories are basically labour-intensive — they rely on swift bulk production by teams of cutters, seam-stitchers, and finishers. Methods are not greatly different from those of a century ago, except that machines are powered.

A typical clothing factory specializes in men's, women's, or children's outerwear, working clothes and uni-

The cutter in a clothing factory first outlines the pattern in chalk, then follows it with an electrically powered cutting knife. He may cut several layers of cloth at a time.

forms, shirts or blouses, overcoats and rainwear, or sports goods — the list of possibilities seems infinite. But basically each depends on the season's range that it devises to attract customers.

Of course, production starts many months before the season for which it is intended — usually a year ahead. Patterns for each size required are cut, materials are ordered from textile mills, orders brought in by sales representatives are analyzed, and production schedules are worked out accordingly.

A typical garment is commenced on the cutting table, where layers of material are stacked one above the other. The top layer is marked in chalk to indicate the cutting pattern. A man's three-piece suit could involve thirty or forty separate components (including lining), and a number of such suits could be fashioned in one cutting operation. The components of a particular suit are labelled with its number so that they can be rematched should they be separated at some point. Most garments are assembled by teams of seam-stitchers, each carrying out one phase of the operation on an electric sewing-machine, until eventually completed garments are pressed and checked.

A major part of the clothing industry in Canada is concerned with raw materials not so common in other countries — particularly leather and fur, which are ideally matched to resist Canada's winters. Garments are produced in Montreal, which is also the centre of the boot and shoe industry.

Dyed yarns are coned for shipment to knitters.

Textiles are either woven (from two sets of yarn) or knitted (with one set). These are circular knitting machines in a mill near Montreal.

47

CHEMICALS

Canada's chemical manufacturing industries are so broad-based that they defy neat categorization. A helpful distinction is between those which process industrial chemicals from raw materials, and those which use these chemicals to make other products.

In assessing chemical feedstocks, there is an immediate division into 'organic' (derived from living matter) and 'inorganic' materials. Organic materials include animal fats, vegetable products, coal, and, most important today, the hydrocarbons petroleum (from decomposed sea creatures) and natural gas (from decomposed vegetation).

Inorganic materials are usually derived from rock minerals, for instance potash, phosphate, and sulphur. Canada has important deposits of a number of potentially valuable inorganic feedstocks, and significant quantities of hydrocarbons. In the course of a century a sophisticated chemical industry has grown up around them.

The first chemical operation in New France was Nicholas Follin's potash and soap factory near Quebec City, licensed in 1674. There potash was leached from wood ashes. Wood-based potash remained a major product in Quebec until late in the nineteenth century. Inorganic minerals like salt, lime, and pyrite were utilized to produce a range of chemical products.

The modern chemical industry came into being with the development of electric furnaces as a means of producing inorganic chemicals in commercial quantities. In this connection, in 1892 the Canadian inventor T. L. Willson developed the world's first commercial process for the production of calcium carbide, the basis of acetylene gas. It was Willson who, after developing hydroelectric potential in Ontario, first utilized the power of the Saguenay river in Quebec, and in 1896 initiated the province's first hydrochemical plant to produce chloralkali. Availability of power remains a major factor in deciding the location of chloralkali plants, though for other producers the proximity of raw materials and markets is more important.

By World War I Canada was exporting industrial chemicals, and was in a position to accept major responsibilities in manufacturing munitions and special chemicals, particularly 'heavy chemicals' (in terms of volume produced) like acids, alkalis, salts, and gases, used as the raw materials of other industries.

At the same time there had been major strides in developing organic chemicals from petrochemical feedstocks, because Canada was cut off from traditional foreign suppliers. In the same way Canada was obliged to develop a 'fine chemicals' industry, processing pharmaceuticals, flavourings, reagents, and other products.

The period between the world wars saw important advances in all fields of chemical production, which not only supplied the manufacturing and construction industries with raw materials but also supplied agriculture with fertilizers and feeds and the mining industry with explosives and the means to beneficiate metals.

There was another surge forward during World War II, and the Canadian government initiated many enterprises, which after the war were transferred to the private sector. These included military explosives manufacture, with the proviso that production was subject to strict government control.

Today both organic and inorganic heavy chemicals are produced across Canada, with an important proportion in

The prilling tower at an ammonium nitrate prill (pellet) plant at McMasterville, near St. Hilaire. Ammonium nitrate prills are used extensively as blasting agents and as fertilizer.

Quebec. In particular Montreal's old position as the centre of oil refineries (for fuel) led to development of petrochemical industries, but using crude materials imported from outside Canada, rather than from the western provinces.

Beyond the manufacture of industrial chemicals is the complex field of 'allied' chemical industries — those that use chemicals as raw materials for further manufacture. These include both consumer products and intermediate chemicals used in other applications, especially metals refining and the pulp and paper and textiles industries. Principal allied chemical industries include fertilizer manufacture (particularly those based on ammonia), coal-tar distillation (to produce tar, creosote, and various chemicals), explosives and ammunition, medicinals, soaps and toilet preparations, paints, varnishes and lacquers, and most impressive of all, the world of plastics.

The chloralkali plant at Bécancour supplies customers in Eastern Canada and the north-eastern United States. Bécancour is on the south bank of the St. Lawrence opposite Trois Rivières.

Explosives are important in the mining and construction industries. This is a blast at a stone quarry in Quebec.

A polyethylene 'bubble,' from which container packaging will be made, is extruded from heated polymer pellets through the action of compressed air.

ELECTRICITY

Among Quebec's great assets is immense hydraulic potential, of which only a portion has so far been utilized. It is the basis of the province's great hydroelectric generating industry, serving the province and its neighbours east, west, and south.

The principle behind hydroelectricity is relatively simple. Falling water is channelled down a penstock to hit the runners (like paddlewheels) of a turbine and set it spinning. The turbine drives a shaft which is connected to a generator. Here huge magnets rotate within wire coils and set up an electric current.

Canada's first known hydroelectric power source, operating by 1885, served Ottawa. Quebec City had one in 1895, Sherbrooke in 1896, and Montreal in 1898 — each time utilizing a power source in the immediate neighbourhood, since it was not yet possible to transmit power effectively over long distances.

The Daniel Johnson dam, part of the Manic-Outardes hydroelectric scheme, was the world's largest multiple-arch dam when it was completed in 1968.

Electrical power was at first a gimmick — a modern means of lighting plants, homes, and eventually streets. But soon electric motors and industrial processes were developed. Electrolytic techniques of smelting aluminum led to the establishment of plants on the St. Maurice river and later on the Saguenay. Another major use of hydroelectricity was to power pulp and paper mills, especially after 1910 when Quebec followed Ontario in banning the export of unprocessed pulpwood. Simple water power had long been used by gristmills and sawmills throughout the south of the province, and many of these also switched to hydroelectricity.

In the early days electricity was generated by industrial users themselves, or by private utility companies serving particular localities. In 1944 the provincial government expropriated two big power operations serving Montreal, and this was the beginning of today's provincially operated Hydro-Quebec.

In 1963 the province acquired the assets of other major suppliers in the province, intending to develop a wide-ranging power grid. Already it had begun expanding rapidly on its own account, since it appeared that in

Engineers test a 735 kV line at Hydro-Quebec's research institute at St. Julie, near Montreal.

An engineer inspects one of the giant turbines in operation at the Shawinigan powerhouse on the St. Maurice river.

were the first such lines to be erected.

The Manicouagan–Outardes scheme was one of the biggest construction projects ever attempted in North America and was a matter of great pride to Quebeckers, since they had brought it into being with a minimum of outside help. The same goes for the huge La Grande project commenced in 1972 in the James Bay region. The La Grande river flows into James Bay near Fort George in the north. Four major generating plants are contemplated, involving not merely huge dams but also a transportation and communications network initiated from scratch. Local native peoples have agreed to waive aboriginal rights in return for substantial cash settlements.

James Bay and other locations in New Quebec hold many more potential sources of hydro power. In addition, Hydro-Quebec buys virtually all the output of Labrador's Churchill Falls scheme, and generates additional electricity by steam (using imported fossil fuels) and nuclear power.

Hydro-Quebec serves its own customers and occasionally has a surplus for export, particularly to New Brunswick and Ontario. The province has arranged to exchange out-of-season surplus power with New York State, where peak electrical use is in summer (for air-conditioning), while Quebec's is in winter (for heating).

Quebec the demand for electricity doubled every ten years. Hydro-Quebec's first major development project involved the two rivers entering the St. Lawrence at Baie Comeau, the Manicouagan and the Outardes. Commenced in 1959, the scheme involved construction of four major generating stations on the Manicouagan (the 'Manics'), and three on the Outardes, together with a number of complex dams.

Two of these developments broke world records. Manic 5, the farthest upstream, involved the world's largest multiple-arch dam. It was named after the Union Nationale premier, Daniel Johnson, when he died there on the eve of its opening in 1968. Earlier, Manic 2 had become the world's largest hollow-joint gravity dam. The Daniel Johnson dam holds back one of the world's great reservoirs, which has a surface area of 1950 km². Power from the various generating stations is transmitted to Quebec City and Montreal on lines capable of operating at 735 kV, which

The Manic–Outardes hydroelectric scheme in Eastern Quebec and the La Grande scheme in the James Bay region enable Hydro-Quebec to keep pace with consumer demand.

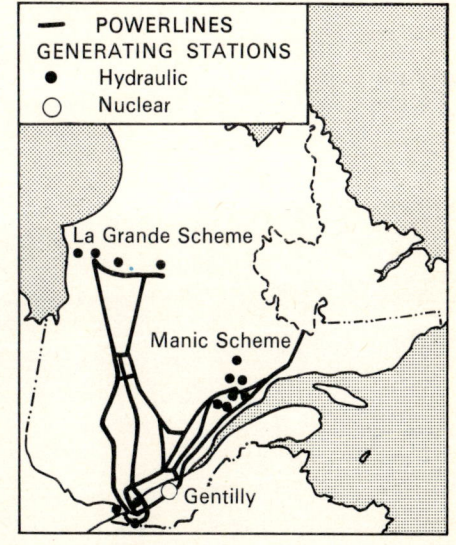

- POWERLINES
GENERATING STATIONS
● Hydraulic
○ Nuclear

La Grande Scheme

Manic Scheme

Gentilly

Fossil Fuels and Uranium

Although Quebec has overwhelming electrical potential, it lacks hydrocarbon fuel — coal, natural gas, and oil, which are traditionally cheap compared with electrical energy, though their rising cost has encouraged Quebec to concentrate increasingly on electricity for energy needs. A government agency conducts a major search for sources of hydro-carbon, but so far only tiny resources of natural gas have been located. The bulk of the province's needs of natural gas have been piped from the western provinces to Montreal. Coal has been imported from the United States and oil from South America.

Rising costs of oil imported from outside Canada make it economic to pipe or ship oil to Quebec from the western provinces, to serve fuel needs and to provide feedstock for Quebec's thriving petrochemical industry. Meanwhile the province prospects for uranium deposits on the Canadian Shield, to provide fuel for nuclear plants.

TRANSPORT

Quebec's early history is indissolubly bound up with the St. Lawrence river, the reason for its foundation. The early settlers and their Indian partners used the river and its tributaries as highways, carrying them throughout the colony.

The river was accessible to ocean craft as far as Hochelaga on Montreal island, at the junction of the Ottawa and St. Lawrence rivers. The Richelieu, navigable to Lake Champlain, entered the St. Lawrence at Sorel, some 40 km downstream, but was much closer by overland portage. Montreal island was a perfect base for trading expeditions north and west, and also for forays south.

Originally Quebec City was the hub of the St. Lawrence transport system, easily accessible to ocean windjammers. Cargoes were transshipped to smaller craft for onward shipment to Montreal, and export lumber from the interior was rafted to Quebec to be loaded. With the development of steam navigation, ocean freighters sailed direct to Montreal.

Montreal's influence steadily increased as colonization spread westward. Most cargoes for and from Europe, and indeed from the south, had to be transshipped there. Much of its significance remains, though the Ottawa and Richelieu are no longer important navigation routes.

However, Montreal today is only one of several ports on the St. Lawrence system, which since the opening of the St. Lawrence Seaway in 1959 has blossomed into one of the world's busiest water routes. It begins with a series of locks immediately upstream of Montreal and extends to Lake Superior. The opening of the Seaway has encouraged development of new ports in Quebec, particularly iron ore terminals at Sept-Iles and Port Cartier on the northern shore of the Gulf of St. Lawrence. Pelletized iron ore is shipped to steelworks in Ontario and the United States by special bulk 'lakers,' or it is exported across the Atlantic.

At Baie Comeau lakers transship cereal exports to ocean freighters bound for Europe. Port Alfred, north on the Saguenay (Baie des Ha! Ha!), handles bauxite and aluminum exports from local smelters. Quebec City's port is

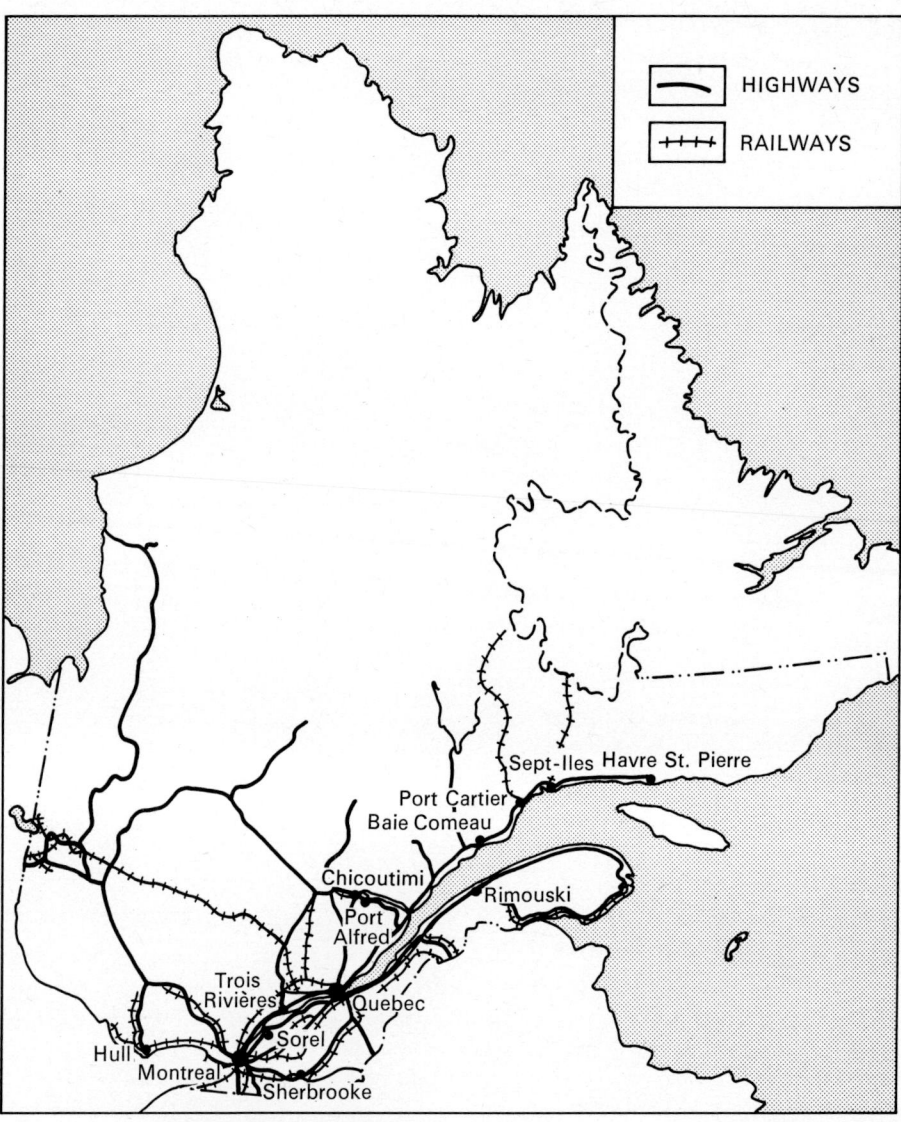

Since the seventeenth century, the St. Lawrence has been Quebec's major highway. It is now lined by a succession of ports linked with inland centres by a comprehensive network of highways and railroads.

Montreal's port remains Canada's most important, though ocean ships bound to and from ports on the Great Lakes may bypass it.

Iron ore companies operating on the Labrador trench transport concentrate to the coast by private railway. Here an iron ore train from Mount Wright passes spectacular scenery on its way to Port Cartier.

The iron ore port of Sept-Iles on the north shore of the St. Lawrence handles more tonnage than any other port in Canada, but its operations are specialized.▼

and passenger service throughout inhabited Quebec. Canadian Pacific's main line from Montreal to the Maritimes cuts a corner and runs through Maine. Independent railways carry iron ore from the interior to ports on the north shore of the St. Lawrence.

The railways have been invaluable in developing Quebec's trade and commerce, but inevitably they have lost ground to the road system, which has improved dramatically since the arrival of the automobile. Quebec's network is well developed in the south and is gradually being extended north. Recent thrusts have carried it to James Bay. The chief route is the Trans-Canada Highway, which crosses Quebec from New Brunswick to Ontario. It takes in both Quebec City and Montreal, but for most of the way it follows the south bank of the St. Lawrence. Another major highway has been developed between the two big cities by way of Trois Rivières.

Several major bridges have been erected to span the St. Lawrence. The Laviolette at Trois Rivières is Quebec's longest — 2 km across. The Pierre Laporte at Quebec City is Canada's longest suspension bridge, and the Lafontaine tunnel-bridge links Montreal island with the south shore of the St. Lawrence.

A laker — designed to fit the minimum dimensions of locks on the Seaway — negotiates the St. Lambert lock near Montreal.

being enlarged following deep dredging, and ports upstream include Trois Rivières and Sorel.

In former times the St. Lawrence was frozen over for five months of the year, producing ice jams and floods. Today, however, ice-breakers keep channels open, and Montreal is accessible to cargo ships with reinforced hulls throughout the winter. An inland container port is in operation both summer and winter.

Long before this became possible, Montrealers relied on an age-old portage route between the St. Lawrence and Lake Champlain in New York, by way of the Richelieu river. Canada's first short railway improved this route, running from Montreal to St. Jean on the lake. It was opened for passengers and goods in 1836.

Other railways were constructed to improve these routes to the south, and again Montreal was the crossroads. In due course it became the eastern terminus for the great cross-continental railroads, which survive today as Canadian Pacific and Canadian National, both headquartered in Montreal. Canadian National's network provides freight

Montreal's Mirabel airport is the world's largest. It was built to ease the pressure on nearby Dorval airport, which had previously served as Canada's international gateway. Now Mirabel handles intercontinental traffic, while Dorval is used by domestic and continental services.

Controllers in the tower at Montreal's Dorval airport monitor incoming and outgoing traffic. Both visual flight rules (VFR) and instrument flight rules (IFR) are in operation.

AIR TRAFFIC

The presence of Air Canada, such international airports as Mirabel and Dorval, and the regional carriers Quebecair and Nordair suggest that all is well with Quebec aviation. Indeed, the International Civil Aviation Organization (ICAO) is headquartered in Montreal.

However, in any society airline traffic amounts to only a small proportion of aviation activity. The great majority is in the sector of 'general aviation,' especially small-craft flying by commercial and private pilots for business or for pleasure. The private pilots in particular form a reservoir on which all aviation depends.

Quebec's reservoir of pilots, however, has been noticeably smaller than in provinces to the west. In 1977 there was only one pilot for each 1000 people in Quebec, against two in Ontario, three in the four western provinces generally, and four in Alberta. There was an appropriately smaller number of aircraft registered in Quebec.

The reasons for the shortfall are partly economic and partly linguistic. Until recently few Quebeckers had the means (or inclination) to take up flying. In any case, Canadian tradition was that only English should be used in ground-air communications, to avoid confusion. The custom automatically excluded Quebeckers who spoke only French.

In 1962 the chief controller at Baie Comeau airport, on the north shore of the St. Lawrence, inquired whether the owner of the local flying school might use French to communicate with a group of unilingual students. Ottawa sent its ruling. Controllers were to speak only English, except in 'emergencies and stress situations.'

Then followed the federal Official Languages Act of 1969, which required that federal services should be available to Canadians in both French and English. At the same time, more Quebeckers were learning to fly, a result of increasing prosperity in the province. There was now a movement to introduce French into the air.

In 1974 the federal Department of Transport sanctioned the use of French at five small Quebec airports under VFR conditions. These apply when pilots can see and avoid each other by 'visual flight rules,' as opposed to IFR (instrument flight rules) used in more complex situations like cloud and night flying.

But for militant francophone pilots and air controllers, the concession was not enough. They formed l'Association des Gens de l'Air du Québec, committed to work for the introduction of French at all airports. Under pressure, the federal Department of Transport agreed to introduce French under VFR at all Quebec

Controllers watch aircraft movements by means of radar. Rigorous safety rules are observed to make sure that aircraft do not collide in the crowded airspace.

Aviation has been a major factor in opening Quebec's remote north. Here a scheduled flight rests at Fort Chimo in Ungava.

airports (including Mirabel and Dorval), and eventually under IFR too, following development of new procedures.

Anglophone pilots and air controllers retaliated. In 1976 CATCA (the Canadian Air Traffic Control Association, some of whose anglophone members, unable to speak French, found their jobs threatened) launched a series of illegal strikes. At the same time CALPA (Canadian Air Line Pilots Association) refused to fly, on the grounds that it was now unsafe to fly over Quebec.

The crisis eased, but not before all francophone Quebeckers rallied to the campaign whether or not they understood its implications. Tens of thousands sported buttons proclaiming: 'Il y a du français dans l'air. . . .' The issue polarized nationalist feeling in Quebec against Ottawa and anglophone Canada so much that it helped the Parti Québécois to win the election in 1976.

Meanwhile, the Department of Transport pressed on with measures to introduce French as demanded. It was recognized that the ICAO expected only

that 'air-ground, radio-telephony communications should be conducted in the language normally used by the station on the ground,' though 'English should be available on request.'

Assuming that the general introduction of French will encourage many more Quebeckers to take up flying, it can only benefit the province. The pilots will want to fly aircraft, the aircraft will help development of the interior, development will lead to more commercial enterprise, and that will lead to more jobs and greater prosperity for all.

COMMUNICATIONS

The French language brackets transportation and communications as 'les échanges,' a helpful concept not available in English. Montreal is traditionally Canada's prime 'exchange,' and in communications maintains a strong lead over other centres.

Modern telecommunications science sprang from experiments in electricity. Samuel Morse invented the telegraph in 1844, and by the end of 1847 several lines were operating in Canada. One ran from Quebec City to Rivière du Loup, a second ran from Quebec to Toronto, a third connected Toronto with the United States.

The system soon embraced all Eastern Canada. It centred on Montreal and communicated through the tapped dots and dashes of Morse code. In 1876 Alexander Graham Bell used a telegraph wire near his father's home in Brantford, Ontario, to test his invention, the telephone. It was designed to transmit the speaking voice.

Like the telegraph, the telephone worked by transmitting electrical signals — in the latter case converting sound waves into electrical impulses, which could be carried by wire. In 1880 the Canadian parliament granted a charter to the Bell Telephone Company of Canada to introduce commercial services throughout the nation.

Today Bell Canada is the country's biggest private enterprise, though since 1909 most of its activities have been confined to Quebec and Ontario. Its century of existence has seen constant technical innovation. Northern Telecom, its manufacturing subsidiary, has been largely responsible, and like Bell Canada it is headquartered in Montreal.

Telephone communications remain Bell's chief business, and electrical wire or cable its chief means of transmission. But a wide range of alternative electrical products are carried too — teleprinted text, photographs and maps, network television and radio transmissions, computer data, and many more.

Its versatility has made communications a major growth industry, especial-

ly because telegraph and telephone technology have gradually profited from wireless dissemination of radio waves. At first confined to coded messages (like the telegraph), wireless was soon utilized to broadcast the spoken word too.

At first radio telephones were used to communicate between ship and shore, though thousands of ham radio operators demonstrated the potential of radio entertainment. The world's first commercial broadcasting station, WXA, or CFCF as it was later renamed, was licensed in Montreal in 1919.

Canadian National Railways of Montreal, already operating a transcontinental telegraph line alongside its track, developed a chain of broadcasting stations across the country starting in 1923, and even introduced radio receivers to its passenger cars. At the same time long-distance subscriber radio telephone service was introduced.

Today, Canadian telecommunications involve a national grid of elec-

Waterproof cable destined for use in a submarine communications link is wound on to a shipping reel in Lachine.

tronic 'highways,' consisting of land wires, underground cables, high frequency radio links, microwave networks, and the Anik domestic satellite system. Each links a transmitting terminal — perhaps a telephone or telex — with a compatible terminal at the other end. The backbone of the grid is the chain of line-of-sight microwave towers which spans Canada. These receive radio signals, strengthen them, and retransmit them to the next tower along, usually about 45 km away. Canada's Anik communications satellites are microwave repeaters in the sky.

Satellites and microwave towers are used to broadcast Canadian television programs across the country and also through much of the north. Most French-language television from the Canadian Broadcasting Commission — Radio-Canada — orginates in Montreal, as do most of its French-language radio programs.

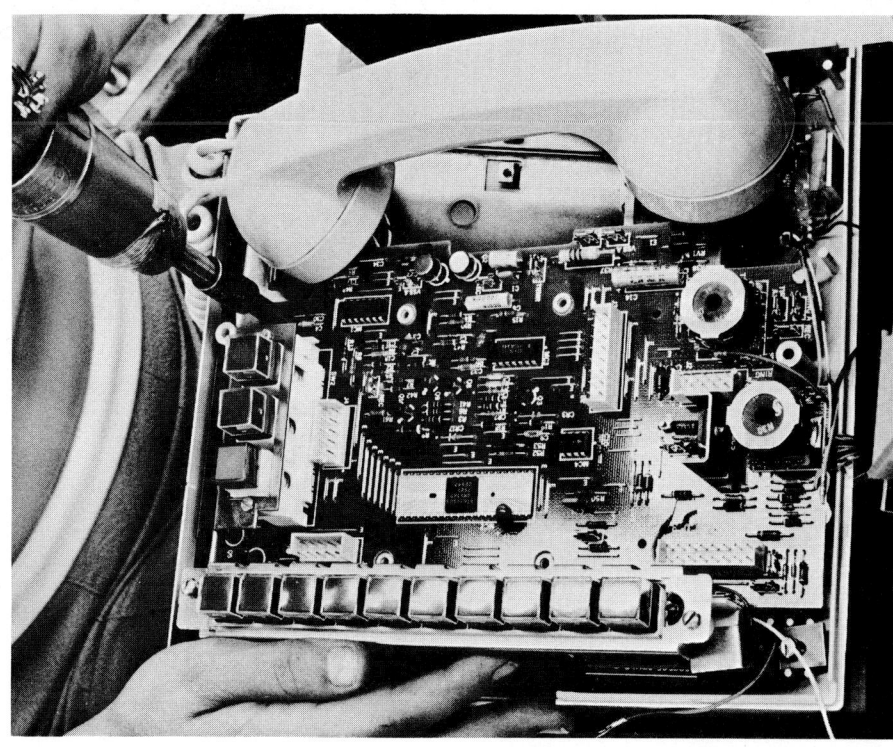

Assembling the electronic circuitry of a telephone set for an SL-I business communications system. Developed in Montreal, the system has been adopted world-wide.

Radio–Canada

The Canadian Broadcasting Commission's French-language arm, Radio-Canada, broadcasts from impressive studio headquarters near Montreal's waterfront. Its television service and that of the rival French network, Télé-Metropole, have achieved great success with Quebec-oriented soap operas or *téléromans*.

The *téléromans* deal with everyday life in Quebec, and have enabled francophone Quebeckers to see themselves and identify with other members of their community throughout the province. They have provided an important element in popular support of Quebec's cultural renaissance.

In addition, the television services provide a French view of news and current affairs. In Radio-Canada's case the programs are broadcast not only throughout Quebec, but also to francophone listeners throughout Canada, over stations owned by the CBC or operated privately under franchise.

Quebec-orientated *téléromans* (soap operas) are very popular in Quebec. Here the production team includes (*from the top*) author, script assistant, producer, sound engineer, and technical director.

Radio-Canada's headquarters in Montreal consists of a hexagonal office tower atop the production facilities. All radio and television production takes place on two levels underground.

MONTREAL

One-third of Quebec's population lives in Montreal, Canada's largest city. The concentration reflects the pre-eminence Montreal has enjoyed since the early days of British occupation, chiefly through its dominance of northern trade routes.

The pre-eminence is ironic, as the city was founded merely as a mission centre — as the great cross on Mount Royal commemorates, replacing the original cross set there by Maisonneuve. But the mission was soon overshadowed by the trading community that gathered around it, which purchased furs from the Indians of the interior.

Montreal grew rich on the proceeds of the fur trade, and shadows of its early opulence linger in the handsome buildings of Old Montreal on the riverfront. The area is slowly being restored to its former grandeur, and Ramezay manor house (1705) and Pierre du Cavalet House (c1770) are examples of what is possible.

Vieux Montréal could be a museum piece, but instead it has maintained a distinct lifestyle of its own. In the daytime streets are thronged with office workers, shoppers, and tourists. At night many fine restaurants and discothèques come into their own, and liveliest of all the *boîtes à chanson,* taverns featuring young entertainers.

Montreal's town hall is in the old city, and so are the new law courts. Due west is the heart of the business district, which helped build Montreal's fortunes and is centred on the tower of the Montreal Stock Exchange.

Many important and world famous Canadian corporations have their headquarters in Montreal, but recent years have seen a steady decline in the city's commercial fortunes. New enterprise has gravitated to Toronto, and old enterprise has stagnated in the face of uncertain political conditions.

Besides, Montreal's former pre-eminence as Canada's chief port has been damaged by the St. Lawrence Seaway. Even so, it is still Canada's transport capital. The two cross-continental railroads have their headquarters in Montreal, and so have Air Canada and Canada Steamship Lines, the nation's biggest shipping company.

Montreal is the world's second biggest French-speaking city after Paris, with a nightlife style to match. Cafés, restaurants, and *boîtes de chanson* keep Old Montreal and the downtown city alive until the early hours of the morning.

Montreal has been overtaken by Metropolitan Toronto as Canada's most populous city, but it has kept pace with it in updating its downtown commercial centre.

Montreal is blessed with a generous number of parks and cool open spaces, such as Dominion Square in the city's heart.

Montrealers remain loyal to French traditions of stylish appearance, and the city is full of clothing boutiques catering to exclusive tastes.

Montreal's economic decline is not confined to big business and transport. Traditionally its major industries have been textiles and clothing, but these are fighting a losing battle against cheap foreign imports. The clothing and footwear industries in particular have lost their hold on Canada's market.

In spite of such setbacks, Montreal remains Canada's most style-conscious community, and more is spent there per head on clothes and cosmetics than anywhere else in North America. Elegant stores along St. Catherine and Sherbrooke streets and in the many fashionable shopping malls opened in recent years cater to all tastes.

After hours, Montreal comes to life with Canada's best restaurants (most of them offering French cuisine) and some fine night spots, as well as a great variety of cultural and musical presentations. Much of this activity takes place in the Place des Arts, completed in 1963 and equipped with three large theatres-cum-auditoriums.

The city has four universities — McGill and Concordia (English-speaking), and Montreal and a campus of the University of Quebec (both French). Among important collections it holds the Quebec National Library, which is the best in the province, the Montreal Museum of Fine Arts, and the Museum of Contemporary Art.

On summer weekends Montrealers frequent the many parks in the city, which include the two summits of Mount Royal and amount to 10 per cent of Montreal's total area. In winter many use the scores of open-air skating rinks provided in these parks. In winter and summer they escape to the nearby Laurentians, Montreal's playground.

Montreal is mostly francophone, but there is great cultural diversity. English-speakers tend to congregate in the city's west end, and are numerous enough to justify two big English daily newspapers (compared with five French). There is a substantial Jewish community, and Italians are much in evidence.

'67 AND '76

Montreal emerged from World War II with the reputation of being one of the most corrupt cities in the western world. Gambling and prostitution thrived, the police force and City Hall were a scandal, and organized crime (*Le Milieu*) was a fact of life.

The situation reflected the major social upheavals that Montreal had experienced during the war — opposition to the establishment crystallized during the conscription crisis. It seemed that the church's worst misgivings about big city life were confirmed, and that Montreal was another Sodom or Gomorra.

In the later 1940s, Duplessis's provincial government tried to stamp out corruption in Montreal through a series of prosecutions. But the city turned a new leaf only when Jean Drapeau was elected mayor in 1954. Pledged to introduce social reform and good government, he set about an energetic campaign to restore Montreal's good name.

Drapeau was defeated in the mayoral race in 1957 after upsetting members of the Duplessis faction, the underworld, and anglophone business interests. But he returned in 1960, and from that time retained power as if he had been born to it. He set in motion a series of *grands projets*, designed to confirm Montreal as a major world city.

Ideas for the projects came from cities which Drapeau visited to discover what they could teach Montreal. Plans to restore Old Montreal were largely based on those employed in New Orleans; Montreal's Metro was designed after study of the subway system in Paris; and the ambitious Place des Arts was planned to match the world's best.

But Drapeau had even greater schemes. One which brought him and Montreal into the minds of all Canadians was Expo 67, the great Universal and International Exhibition commissioned to celebrate Canada's centennial year. With exhibits from all over the world, Expo attracted 50 million visitors from home and overseas. The exhibition was an enormous success. For the first time all Canada came to feel proud of a home-grown achievement, and realized that the nation (and Montreal, its biggest

city) could stage an event of worldwide significance. Montreal's old reputation as a city of vice and corruption was forgotten.

Then Drapeau achieved what should have proved an even greater coup — persuading the International Olympic Committee to stage the 1976 Summer Games in Montreal. However, rising nationalist feeling in Quebec had alienated Canadians in other provinces, and even in Montreal there was only limited enthusiasm.

Construction for the Games involved enormous capital outlay, and from the beginning the event was overshadowed by worries over who was to foot the bill. Besides, there were allegations of corruption in the handling of contracts, and labour troubles were so severe that it seemed impossible that construction could be finished in time.

The Olympic Park in Montreal's east end remains a memorial to the 1976 Olympic Games, but the arena is used today by the Montreal Alouettes and the Montreal Expos. This is how it looked during the Olympics' closing ceremony.

Expo 67's exhibition grounds were constructed on a man-made island in the St. Lawrence. Some of the buildings survive to house the cultural exhibition 'Man and his World,' open every summer.

The Place des Arts is a three-in-one concert centre of international stature.

Eventually the Quebec provincial government took over the construction program — insisting that the Olympics were Quebec's, not Canada's. The rest of the country anticipated a fiasco. As it turned out the Games ran with scarcely a hitch, but without producing the profit that Drapeau had expected.

Montreal was left with Olympic facilities (including the unfinished tower in the Olympic Stadium) and a demand that the city pay a large share of the cost. This left further hard feelings, but the installations are well patronized. The stadium is the home arena of the Montreal Alouettes (football) and the Montreal Expos (baseball).

The Expo site, meanwhile, has become a permanent cultural exhibition celebrating 'Man and His World.' It continues to attract curious visitors in great numbers. But Montreal's current needs are more mundane — municipal housing, and on the metropolitan level, sewage treatment and an improved transport infrastructure. For the time these have taken precedence over further grand schemes to make Montreal 'the city of tomorrow.'

Regional Goverment

The Quebec provincial government delegates regional administration to local authorities, particularly municipalities governed by mayor and council who administer revenue derived from property taxes, government taxes, and various taxes on sales and industry. Today municipalities are being grouped together in the interests of greater efficiency.

Besides municipalities, however, since 1970 Quebec has had three 'supramunicipalities' in the major centres of Montreal, Quebec City, and Hull. These are termed 'urban communities,' and the amalgamation makes it possible to combine certain intermunicipal services, co-ordinating efforts and distributing responsibilities fairly.

The Quebec Urban Community includes twenty-six distinct municipalities and Hull's includes eight, though much of its loyalty is directed to the National Capital Commission, which brackets it with Ottawa across the river. Each urban community is served by a council consisting of one representative from each municipality, usually its mayor.

Montreal's, however, is served by a council consisting of the seven members of Montreal City Council's executive committee (including Montreal's mayor), and one representative each from twenty-eight other municipalities under the urban community's jurisdiction.

As mayor of Montreal, Jean Drapeau brought about Expo 67, the 1976 Olympic Games, and many other 'grands projets' which changed the face of the city.

Old Quebec is walled, as it was two centuries ago. The wall is pierced by several gates which lead to the picturesque streets of the old city.

QUEBEC CITY

Unlike English-speaking Quebeckers, francophones have no difficulty in distinguishing Quebec the province and Quebec the city. In French the province is preceded by the definite article (*le Québec*) but the city is not.

The English, however, refer to it as 'Quebec City.' In contrast with Montreal it is nearly 100 per cent French and, in spite of vigorous attempts to promote it as a tourist centre, it remains relatively unknown to travellers. This is sad, for Quebec is Canada's birthplace, one of the most fascinating places in all North America.

Those tourists who do reach Quebec make a beeline for the Old City, the only walled community in North America apart from one or two in Mexico. Ironically, its most distinctive features are relatively recent — the Citadel, now headquarters of the famous *'Van Doos'* (Royal 22nd Regiment), and the Château Frontenac hotel.

But more penetrating investigation reveals buildings far older and with much greater historic significance. The usual city tour begins in the 'Upper Town' where most of these buildings are situated. A more appropriate beginning would be to start with the 'Lower Town' of Place Royale, which is where Champlain established his *habitation*.

In the years that followed the first settlement of 1608 many houses were built in the Lower Town, but all were destroyed in a fire of 1682, and only traces of walls survive in the basements of present structures. In 1688 the first stone was laid at the site of Notre Dame des Victoires church, which was once occupied by Champlain's house.

Throughout the eighteenth century Place Royale was a market place and the busiest part of the town, but following Wolfe's victory of 1759 there was a steady move to the Upper Town. Lower Town has remained largely untouched since those days, and the Quebec government is taking steps to restore the old atmosphere.

Quebec Citadel is garrisoned by the famous Royal 22nd Regiment, the 'Van Doos.' Here they parade their regimental colours.

The Upper Town and the Plains of Abraham beyond are so full of history that it takes days to explore them properly. Merely to walk in Old Quebec is to step back centuries, but it is well worth trying to complete the pedestrian tour suggested by the city's tourist authority. This takes in all the most fascinating locations.

Perhaps the most interesting sites are the Hôtel Dieu (1639), North America's oldest hospital north of Mexico; the Convent of the Ursulines (1639), Canada's oldest institution for the education of women, where Montcalm's remains are preserved; and the Seminaire de Québec (1663), founded by Bishop Laval who was buried there.

Old Quebec is full of stories, but it has a modern life too. Its shops, and even more its restaurants, are most attractive. Fortunately it has been shielded from the major developments beyond the city walls, which have transformed the rest of the community.

Today, Greater Quebec extends all the way up the St. Lawrence river to Ste. Foy, taking in a series of modern highrise office blocks stretching back from the Gothic buildings of the National Assembly which occupy the highest vantage point. Many of the blocks house departments of the Quebec provincial civil service, the city's chief employer.

The city is a significant river port and is slowly succeeding in building up local industry, which serves its immediate area and the hinterland beyond. But inevitably most economic activity is concerned with the provincial government, the tourist industry, trade and distribution to the wide area around Quebec City, and the region's agriculture.

As a cultural centre, Quebec is strong. There are several museums, including the Quebec Museum. There are two universities, Laval (1852) and a campus of the University of Quebec (both French medium), and a number of community colleges. There are several theatres, particularly Le Grand Théâtre de Québec, and a symphony orchestra.

Break-Neck Stairs and Sous-le-Fort Street lead to the oldest quarter of Quebec City, Place Royale, where Champlain built his *habitation.*

A view of Quebec City from the air above Lévis, across the St. Lawrence river. There is a clear distinction between the upper city, dominated by the Château Frontenac, and the lower city on the waterfront.

QUIET REVOLUTION

Throughout their history francophone Quebeckers have been encouraged to respect strong, conservative government. Often this has reached a state of autocracy, as in the days of the French kings, the early British governors, and the regime of Maurice Duplessis. Such governments have generally been supported by leaders of the Roman Catholic church, to ensure the continued *survivance* of Quebec culture and traditions, and to stave off threatened assimilation by the English-speaking world, which surrounds Quebec east, west, and south.

Until World War II the church was both omnipresent and omnipotent in the Quebec situation. But as in many other parts of the world, the basis of society in Quebec changed irreversibly during the war. Labour patterns altered, expectations in life were raised, and individual independence was stressed at the expense of traditional family ties.

The church found itself in difficulties, since it was unable to adjust to the demands of the new society because its structure and precepts had changed little in four centuries. In rural areas the church could hold its own, but in cities and towns ordinary Quebeckers slipped from the grasp of their priests and scorned the church's demands.

Duplessis boasted that 'the bishops ate from his hand,' in spite of a major row with Mgr. Joseph Charbonneau of Montreal following the Asbestos strike. But already within the church there was a feeling that change was essential, particularly social change. The movement had centred on ecclesiastical sociologists at Laval University in Quebec.

Laval's school of social studies had been formed in the 1930s, and many of its students now became prominent in Quebec (and national) politics. When Duplessis died in 1959, there was an immediate outburst of frenzied social reform initiated first by his successors in the Union Nationale, then by Jean Lesage's Liberals elected in 1960.

The Lesage government carried through major reforms in education, labour relations (by allowing public employees to form unions and to resort to industrial action), and social affairs. Following the social principles developed at Laval, the new government aimed to grant control of educational and social agencies to the communities they served.

At the same time, but with no direct connection, there had been a growing independence movement in Quebec. Several small parties were formed during the 1960s to achieve separation from the rest of Canada. The Ralliement National offered candidates in the 1966 election, when the Lesage government was defeated by the Union Nationale.

The National Assembly meets in this chamber. Above the President's chair is Charles Huot's painting of Lower Canada's assembly meeting in 1793.

In 1967 — the centenary of Canada's Confederation — General Charles de Gaulle, President of France, proclaimed in Montreal: 'Vive le Québec libre!' In the same year Liberal squabbles led to the defection of René Lévesque, a former Lesage minister, who formed a new separatist alliance.

Lévesque proposed that Quebec should be a sovereign state enjoying economic interdependence with the rest of Canada. In 1968 his movement was renamed the 'Parti Québécois,' and it became a focal point for all Quebec separatists including most of the Ralliement National. Its efforts won several seats in the Quebec election of 1970.

On that occasion the Liberals under Robert Bourassa ousted the Union Nationale. That party promptly collapsed, so that in 1974 Bourassa won an overwhelming majority in the National Assembly. He used it to introduce further controversial legislation, particularly educational measures which proved unpopular and lost him much support.

In 1976 Bourassa called an election for November 15, on the grounds that he needed a mandate to renegotiate Quebec's place in Confederation. There had been suspicion of corruption in the government, and voters set out to teach the Liberals a lesson. But few supposed they would be beaten. However, the Parti Québécois emerged with a landslide victory — to its own surprise.

During their campaign the *Péquistes* (members of the Parti Québécois) had stressed the need for return to efficiency and integrity in government — a reference to administrative mishaps and scandals which had plagued the Bourassa government — but had underplayed references to secession. In office they moved quickly to make good their election promises of better service, but at the same time they initiated an ambitious legislative program designed to bolster the French language in Quebec. This was at the expense of English, particularly in the spheres of business and government and in schools. The measures helped clear the way for a province-wide referendum on whether Quebec should stay within Canada or leave Confederation.

Ministers of the Crown, including Quebec's prime minister, sit on the President's right in the National Assembly. Here prime minister René Lévesque addresses the House.

Prime Ministers

Since Confederation most Quebec governments have been drawn from the Liberal (L) and Conservative (C) parties, but from 1936, election contests were between the Liberals and the Union Nationale (UN). The Parti Québécois (PQ) first offered candidates in 1970. This is a list of Quebec premiers (prime ministers) to date.

P. J. Chauveau (C)	1867–1873
Gideon Ouimet (C)	1873–1874
C. E. Boucher (C)	1874–1878
H. G. Joly de Lotbinière (L)	1878–1879
Adolphe Chapleau (C)	1879–1882
J. A. Mousseau (C)	1882–1884
John Ross (C)	1884–1887
Louis-Olivier Taillon (C)	1887
Honoré Mercier (L)	1887–1891
C. E. Boucher (C)	1891–1892
Louis-Olivier Taillon (C)	1892–1896
E. J. Flynn (C)	1896–1897
F. G. Marchand (L)	1897–1900
S. N. Parent (L)	1900–1905
Lomer Gouin (L)	1905–1920
L. A. Taschereau (L)	1920–1936
Adelard Godbout (L)	1936
Maurice Duplessis (UN)	1936–1939
Adelard Godbout (L)	1939–1944
Maurice Duplessis (UN)	1944–1959
Paul Sauvé (UN)	1959–1960

Antonio Barrette (UN)	1960
Jean Lesage (L)	1960–1966
Daniel Johnson (UN)	1966–1968
J. J. Bertrand (UN)	1968–1970
Robert Bourassa (L)	1970–1976
René Lévesque (PQ)	1976–

Gouin

Mercier

Duplessis

Taschereau

NATIONAL ASSEMBLY

Following the lead of other provinces, in 1968 Quebec abolished the upper house of its two-chamber legislature. The lower house, consisting of elected representatives of the people, was grandly renamed Quebec's National Assembly.

The name (and what it implied) helped to erase painful memories of what Quebeckers still refer to as 'le conquêt,' after which the French administration and governing style gave way to the British form. In 1793 the creation of Lower Canada had given rise to Quebec's first elected assembly, part of a two-chamber parliament. The elected representatives formed the lower house of the legislature, while representatives nominated by the Crown sat in the upper house — institutions just like the House of Lords and the House of Commons in Britain.

The notion of representative government was a novelty to Canadians, for

The National Assembly in Quebec City was completed in 1886, and was designed to house not only the legislature but also all government departments. However, the under France all power had belonged to the monarch. However, francophone delegates took to parliamentary practice with alacrity, as Charles Huot's painting in the National Assembly commemorates. It shows Chartier de Lotbinière addressing Lower Canada's legislative assembly on January 21, 1793, on the question of equal language rights of French and English.

The legislatures of Upper and Lower Canada combined in 1840 and went on to merge with those of other provinces under the British North America Act of 1867. The act set up Quebec's first provincial legislature, whose twin chambers first met on December 27, 1867. This was the ancestor of today's National Assembly.

Besides restructuring the legislative body, Quebec revised its nomenclature to reflect contemporary practice in the francophone world — more precisely, to that in continental France. Elected rep-

administration has long since outgrown the quarters allotted to it, and has expanded to fill the extensive *cité parlementaire* **on the hill behind.**

resentatives were already 'deputies,' the Speaker who presided over sittings became the 'President,' the Clerk of the Assembly who prepares the Assembly's agenda and is responsible for its minutes (votes and proceedings) became the 'Secretary.'

At the same time, a parliamentary commission considered means of revising Assembly procedure. It aimed to make its rules 'relevant to a modern and efficient parliament where it is possible for the majority to see its legislation adopted, the Opposition to speak without restraint, public opinion to be heard, and finally, every Member to exercise his role as legislator.'

The result was the *Code Lavoie*, the Standing Orders of the National Assembly which were adopted unanimously in 1973 and which greatly simplified the Quebec parliamentary process. An important innovation was a procedure by which interested groups could present evidence to a parliamentary standing committee, following a bill's first reading.

There have been standing committees in the Quebec parliament since 1867, set up to examine legislation in detail on behalf of the whole house. Today there are sixteen of them, one of which is a co-ordinating body appointing members to the others, which each deal with a major area of government responsibility. Each committee consists of about fifteen members drawn from different parties in proportion to their strength in the House.

Individuals and groups present evidence to the committee, which may terminate proceedings when it feels that it has heard enough. However, the measure does make possible a kind of provincial mini-referendum on important issues, by which the views of the public may be sought. Indeed, it is more detailed than a referendum, in that questions may be answered with more than a 'Yes' or 'No.'

The standing committee subsequently reports back to the Assembly as a bill comes up for its second reading. The bill is then considered by the standing committee or by the 'Committee of the Whole' (in effect, the Assembly sitting under more flexible rules), which may recommend amendments.

The bill is then brought before the House for its third reading. If it passes, it must be signed by the provincial lieutenant-governor as representative of the Queen before it becomes law.

Parliamentary committees may hear public briefs concerning proposed legislation. The committees meet in the Assembly's old

Council chamber, decorated in red in the style of the British House of Lords.

Above the main door of the National Assembly is carved 'Je me souviens' (I remember), which has become Quebec's motto. Above it stand statues of James Wolfe (*left*) and Montcalm (*right*).

Cité Parlementaire

Quebec's château-style National Assembly building was built between 1877 and 1886, designed by the architect Eugène Taché, and engineered by Pierre Gauvreau. It was designed to house not only the chambers of the two legislative bodies, but also the offices of all government departments existing at the time.

Since then, public services everywhere have expanded, and now wield so much power that students of political science suggest that they amount to a fourth arm of government in addition to the traditional legislature (parliament itself), executive (in Quebec, the lieutenant-governor-in-council), and judiciary (the courts).

To accommodate Quebec's administration, a whole 'city of parliament' has grown up on the hill above the old city, and the Assembly itself is dominated by the highrise 'G' block, which many contemporary Quebeckers consider a serious architectural *faux-pas*. The 'city' holds some 10 000 civil servants, and the provincial government is Quebec City's chief employer.

In spite of the competition, the National Assembly building more than holds its own. It is a favourite goal for caleche-borne tourists, who are fascinated by the legion of larger-than-life statues that decorate its facade. They represent a score of the great figures of Quebec's past — governors, soldiers, adventurers, and missionaries who symbolize the province's great heritage.

CIVIL CODE

According to the British North America Act, criminal law is a federal matter, but it is for Canada's provinces to set their own civil laws. Most provinces follow English common law, but Quebec has a written civil code.

Originally, New France's *code civile* was adopted wholesale from the code observed in Paris since 1510, and this was declared to be the 'law of Canada' in 1663. As years passed sections of it were abolished, but in their place Canada was subjected to ordinances of the king and his counsel and local ordinances of the intendants.

Following the English occupation of 1760, the Quebec Act of 1774 enshrined the position of 'Canadian law.' This kept it alive beyond the introduction of the Napoleonic Code throughout much of Europe, which took the place of the old regional civil law codes evolved over many centuries.

In 1857 it was decided to recodify the civil law of Lower Canada to take into account the many social and political changes that had occurred over two centuries. A number of eminent jurists were commissioned to prepare the recodification. They drew liberally on the content of the old 'Coutume de Paris' and other coded systems, but followed the form and spirit of the Napoleonic Code and a similar code subsequently prepared in Louisiana with local variations.

The result was a twofold effort — the *Code Civile* and the *Code de Procédure Civile*, each translated into English, though in many cases using the terms of Scottish law rather than the true English system. The bulk of these two codes was introduced in 1866, and in spite of important amendments most elements still stand.

Certainly the general divisions of the Civil Code itself have survived unchanged. It is divided into four books. The first is 'Of Persons' and deals with such matters as enjoyment and loss of civil rights, domicile, marriage, paternal authority, minority and majority, and corporations.

The second is 'Of Property, of Ownership, and of its Different Modifications.' It deals with ownership, usufruct (use and habitation), the distinction

A Quebec provincial court hears a civil action, according to the rules of the Civil Code.

of things, real servitudes, and emphyteusis (perpetual rights in a piece of another's land). The third book is 'Of the Acquisition and Exercise of Rights of Property,' which deals with successions, gifts *inter vivos* (among the living) and by will, obligations, marriage covenants, sale, exchange, lease and hire, partnership, and transactions. The fourth book covers ground which was included in the French system in a separate 'Code of Commerce.'

Like other provinces, Quebec is entitled to administer both civil and criminal justice within the province. In civil matters involving sums greater than $3000, the court of first instance is the Quebec Superior Court, where a single judge presides (with a jury if requested, to decide on matters of fact).

From the Superior Court there is the right of appeal to the Quebec Supreme Court, appellate division. Beyond this stage there may be appeal to the Supreme Court of Canada in Ottawa. Justices of both the Quebec Superior Court and the Supreme Court are appointed by the federal government.

The Supreme Court also includes an assize division, from which justices regularly visit regions of the province to hear serious criminal cases. Usually the judge sits with a jury. Less important matters — civil or criminal — are heard by district or municipal courts, where

The Quebec Supreme Court is housed in Quebec City's *Palais de Justice*. The palace houses many lower courts as well, and is the headquarters of the Quebec judiciary.

judges are appointed by the province's lieutenant-governor. These lesser courts may be provincial (in civil matters involving sums of less than $3000) or Sessions of the Peace, hearing less serious criminal cases. Small-claims courts deal with petty civil cases, in which the parties represent themselves, and social welfare courts deal particularly with juvenile matters.

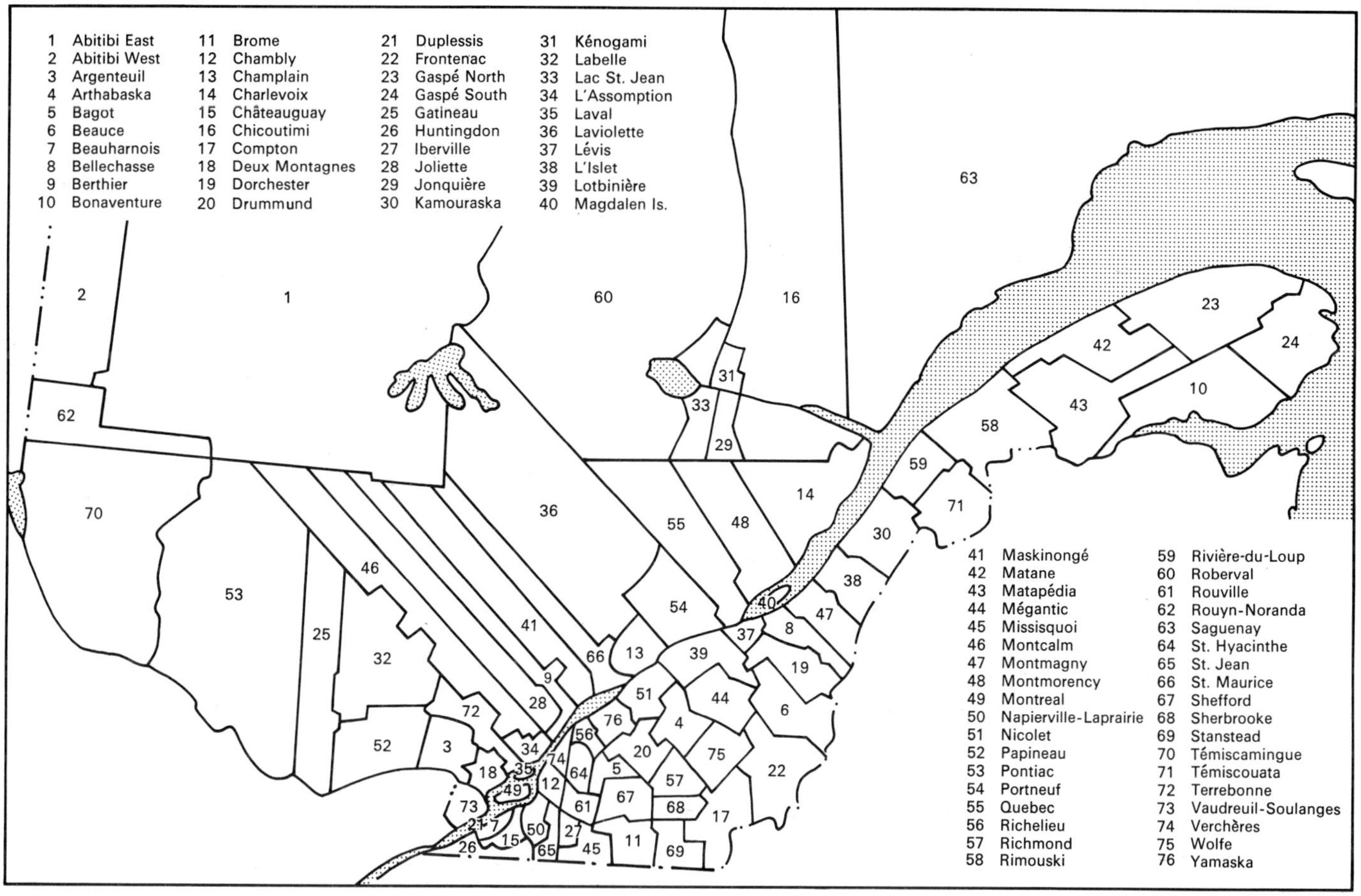

1	Abitibi East	11	Brome	21	Duplessis
2	Abitibi West	12	Chambly	22	Frontenac
3	Argenteuil	13	Champlain	23	Gaspé North
4	Arthabaska	14	Charlevoix	24	Gaspé South
5	Bagot	15	Châteauguay	25	Gatineau
6	Beauce	16	Chicoutimi	26	Huntingdon
7	Beauharnois	17	Compton	27	Iberville
8	Bellechasse	18	Deux Montagnes	28	Joliette
9	Berthier	19	Dorchester	29	Jonquière
10	Bonaventure	20	Drummund	30	Kamouraska

31	Kénogami
32	Labelle
33	Lac St. Jean
34	L'Assomption
35	Laval
36	Laviolette
37	Lévis
38	L'Islet
39	Lotbinière
40	Magdalen Is.

41	Maskinongé	59	Rivière-du-Loup
42	Matane	60	Roberval
43	Matapédia	61	Rouville
44	Mégantic	62	Rouyn-Noranda
45	Missisquoi	63	Saguenay
46	Montcalm	64	St. Hyacinthe
47	Montmagny	65	St. Jean
48	Montmorency	66	St. Maurice
49	Montreal	67	Shefford
50	Napierville-Laprairie	68	Sherbrooke
51	Nicolet	69	Stanstead
52	Papineau	70	Témiscamingue
53	Pontiac	71	Témiscouata
54	Portneuf	72	Terrebonne
55	Quebec	73	Vaudreuil-Soulanges
56	Richelieu	74	Verchères
57	Richmond	75	Wolfe
58	Rimouski	76	Yamaska

The counties of Quebec, delineated for judicial purposes, also serve as electoral districts for provincial elections.

Quebec's Civil Code is contained in a relatively slim volume — a revision of the extensive recodification made in 1857.

The FLQ Crisis

Quebeckers traditionally solve their problems with neighbours by means of peaceful negotiation. It was a shock when in October 1970 young terrorists in Montreal kidnapped James Cross, the British trade commissioner, and made a number of demands related to their organization, the *Front de Libération du Québec* (FLQ).

When the federal government failed to respond, the FLQ kidnapped a Quebec minister, Pierre Laporte. The federal government allowed the FLQ manifesto to be broadcast, but then refused to abide by other conditions. Instead prime minister Pierre Trudeau sent in the army and invoked the War Measures Act.

These measures allowed arrest and detention without a charge, and search without a warrant. The day after the declaration Pierre Laporte was found dead. In the weeks that followed the terrorists lay low, but more than 500 people were detained and thousands more were searched. James Cross was released in December, but only when the federal government agreed to provide safe passage for the kidnappers to Cuba.

Canadians feared that the events prefaced more violence in Quebec and expected the worst. Instead most Quebeckers — including most separatists — deplored what had happened, which conformed to the pattern of political kidnappings then occurring in other countries. In Quebec the events were isolated and have not been repeated.

Police work has many facets. Here officers of the Quebec police recover a sawed-off shotgun from the St. Lawrence river.

EDUCATION

Before the Quiet Revolution of the 1960s, education of francophone Quebeckers rested mainly with the church. Secular clergy organized elementary schools in town and country, and religious orders ran *collèges classiques* and universities.

The traditional progress of a bright pupil was to attend elementary school until twelve years old, then spend eight years at a *collège classique* before proceeding to the university to which it was affiliated — Laval in Quebec City or Montreal or Sherbrooke. Curricula were designed to produce churchmen, advocates, notaries, and doctors.

These four professions had been important when the system was founded but failed to fulfill the needs of modern society. In the 1950s *collèges classiques* and francophone universities introduced scientific studies as well as the humanities, but many students wanting special qualifications were obliged to enter the English system. This was organized along lines familiar elsewhere in Canada, with local school boards controlling elementary and high schools. Graduates proceeded to autonomous universities like McGill in Montreal — founded in 1821 and one of the best in North America — or outside Quebec.

The French system, in contrast, was governed by a 'council of public education,' consisting of Quebec's bishops. Its chief function was to send out inspectors who ensured that standards of instruction — particularly religious instruction — were maintained. On the local level, *commissions scolaires* including priests and laity decided school policy.

The Liberal government of Jean Lesage commissioned a study of education in Quebec, headed by Mgr. Alphonse-Marie Parent, vice-rector of Laval University. Its recommendations led to the establishment of a Department of Education in Quebec in 1964 and to the expropriation of all public school buildings to the province.

Universities and private schools remained autonomous, though they received substantial operating grants from the government. But the character of confessional (Roman Catholic) school boards changed. Now they operated like

Laval University in Ste. Foy, near Quebec City, is an offshoot of the Seminary of Quebec founded by Bishop Laval. The University has twenty faculties, and is regarded as French Canada's leading educational institution.

Quebec schools lay great emphasis on physical training. Here youngsters learn the elements of lacrosse.

non-confessional boards, acting in the interests of the local community rather than on instructions from the bishops.

In pressing the legislation, the Lesage government induced the bishops to agree to support the reforms, after guaranteeing that religious instruction would be continued in confessional schools. That this instruction survives is a reflection of the will of parents in the particular community — basically a cultural consideration.

The public education system which emerged from the reforms was broadly similar to those in other provinces. Children may attend kindergarten, then elementary school from age six and normally for six or at most seven years, then secondary or high school for four or five years. From that point (Grade 12) students may continue to college and perhaps university.

The new college system was set up in 1967, with General and Vocational Colleges (CEGEPs) replacing the old *collèges classiques*. These lead on to full university courses or provide career-oriented courses in their own right, for instance in mechanics, nursing, or graphic design.

Since 1970 there have been major efforts to strengthen the position of French as the medium of instruction in Quebec. The Bourassa government of Liberals came to grief in 1976 after attempting to oblige non-English-speaking immigrants to Quebec to send their children to francophone schools, on the principle that French was Quebec's first language. More controversial still, the Parti Québécois government, which succeeded Bourassa's, quickly proposed legislation by which all newcomers to Quebec (with few exceptions, even if

English-speaking) would be obliged to send their children to French schools. This suggested to some that the Parti Québécois hoped to use the education system to assimilate non-francophone Quebeckers into the French community.

However, in spite of the new legislation many English-medium schools still receive public support. Most of these schools are in the Montreal region and in the Eastern Townships where most anglophones are located, and they are administered as part of the provincial school system along with French-medium schools. Regardless of language, they may be Protestant or Catholic and are served by separate school boards.

Since the passing of Bill 101 in 1977, students at public schools in Quebec have been obliged to study in French, except in special cases where they are permitted to attend English-medium institutions.

Universities

Quebec has six private universities and the publicly incorporated University of Quebec, which has subsidiary university centres in a number of cities and corresponds to state universities in the United States.

Of the private universities, the longest established is McGill University in Montreal, founded through a legacy of the philanthropist James McGill and chartered in 1821. It consists of twelve faculties and several schools, most of which are situated in

Montreal, though the faculty of agriculture, Macdonald College, is west of the city.

Laval University, in Ste. Foy near Quebec City, is an offshoot of the *Seminaire de Québec* founded by Bishop Laval. The university itself was founded in 1852 and has twenty faculties. The University of Montreal was founded in 1878 as a branch of Laval, but was chartered as a university in its own right in 1920.

Like Laval and Montreal, the University of Sherbrooke is French-medium. It was founded in 1954. Bish-

op's University, an English-medium establishment of the Anglican church, is in Lennoxville, which is 5 km from Sherbrooke. Concordia University in Montreal is the result of a merger of two separate universities and is also English-medium.

The University of Quebec has its headquarters in Quebec City and university centres in Montreal, Trois Rivières, Chicoutimi, and Rimouski. It has additional campuses in Hull and Rouyn.

SOCIAL AFFAIRS

The foundations of Quebec's health and social services were laid by religious orders. The hospitals of New France were founded by communities of sisters, and orders like the Ursulines took in foundlings and where possible arranged adoptions.

Until the election of the Lesage government in 1960, it was the tradition in Quebec that health care and welfare services were essentially charitable rather than a matter of public responsibility. Not only Roman Catholic hospitals but many Protestant establishments too were run by autonomous religious orders supported by donations and endowments. A few English hospitals had been organized by lay bodies and were administered as corporations like hospitals elsewhere in Canada. But government presence in the health field was limited to a chain of regional 'health units' set up during the Depression, which were intended to watch for and guard against contagious diseases.

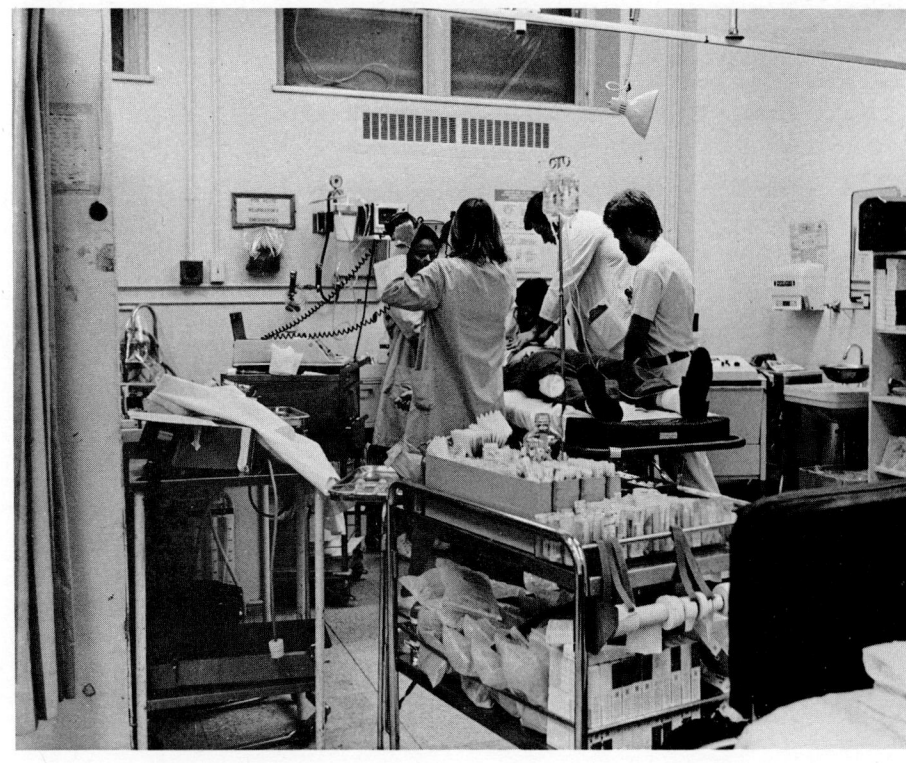

The cardiac arrest team in a hospital emergency department provides immediate aid for a newly arrived patient.

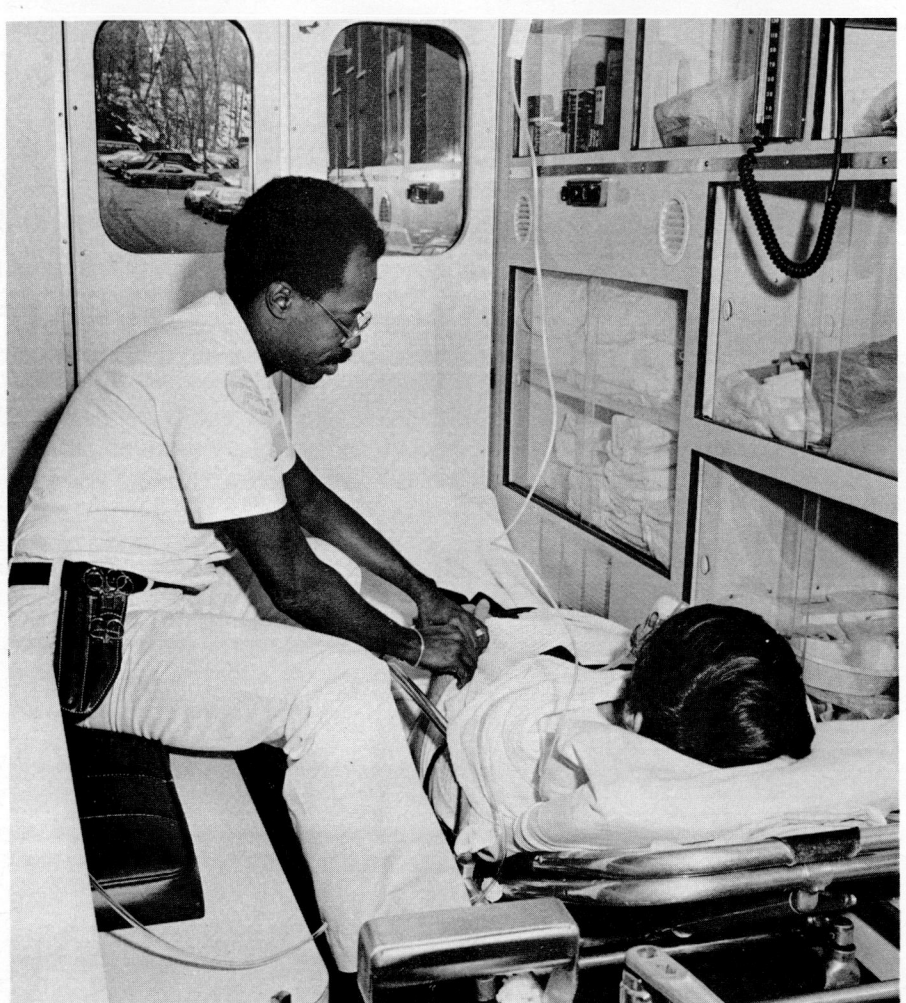

A patient is rushed to Montreal's Royal Victoria Hospital by ambulance. Attendants are trained to cope with every emergency.

In the social field, public assistance had been the province of the secular clergy in New France, and the tradition continued under the English administration. Eventually the federal government introduced social insurance schemes like family allowances, unemployment benefits, and old age pensions. Gaps were supposed to be filled by municipalities, sharing the cost of schemes with the provincial government. In practice much of the work was done by volunteer agencies, and there was great inconsistency across the province, as there was in available health services, in spite of government subsidies to hospitals.

Following Duplessis's death in 1959, the Union Nationale government commissioned a study of hospital services parallel to a separate study of welfare schemes. Before the commissions could report, however, the Lesage Liberal government was elected. It was committed to introduce hospital insurance, taking advantage of a federal offer to share costs.

Meanwhile, Quebec was battling Ottawa over responsibilities for administering the various public assistance schemes. Quebec insisted that they were a provincial matter and that prov-

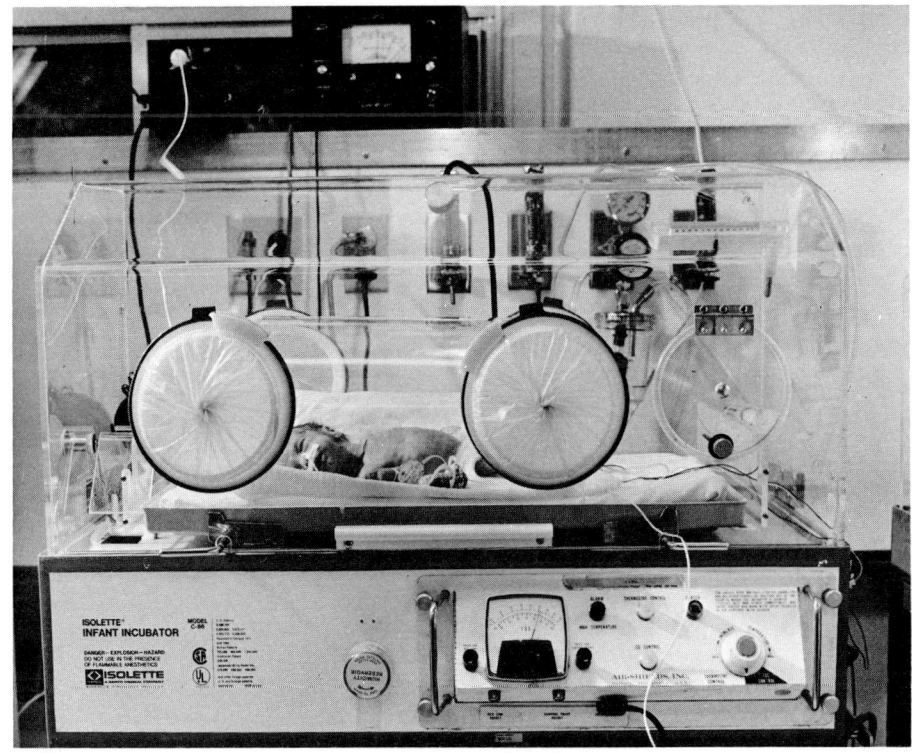

In a hospital's nursery, a premature baby is nursed in an incubator.

inces should have the right to collect the revenue that would compensate for them. The two sides worked out a compromise agreement, and the schemes were implemented.

Quebec's Quiet Revolution was now in full swing, and it had reached the hospitals. Many remained under the control of religious orders, though these were now almost entirely dependent on government subsidies for their existence. But it was a shock when in 1966 lay hospital workers called a general strike when negotiating a new labour contract. The strike was the first crisis to face the new Union Nationale government elected in 1966. Its members were challenged, too, by the federal government's commitment to introduce medicare across Canada. The province commissioned a general study of health and social matters in Quebec, headed by Claude Castonguay, an actuary.

The commission's terms of reference became so general that they came to embrace every aspect of social affairs. Even before its final reports were published, Castonguay himself was elected to the Quebec National Assembly in 1970, and joined the Liberal cabinet as Minister of Health and Family and Social Welfare. This meant that he could implement his own recommendations.

Castonguay's first step was to introduce universal health insurance, a logi-

Before an operation in the operating theatre, the patient is given a general anaesthetic.

cal counterpart to the hospital insurance scheme. The two programs cover all residents of Quebec for any medically necessary services by a physician, dental surgery in university and hospital centres, certain optical services, and all hospital and outpatient clinic costs.

In 1970 Castonguay brought about the amalgamation of the two ministries he headed — Health and Family and Social Welfare respectively — as an integrated Department of Social Affairs. He hoped to co-ordinate Quebec's policies in three fields necessarily closely related — health care, social services, and income security.

In 1972 the Quebec government passed a major bill, by which the many independent agencies working in the health and social fields were reorganized on a regional basis. Eleven regional health and social service councils were established to liaise between the government, the public, the hospitals, and other agencies involved.

Social services were to be evenly spread across the province. In particular, all regions were to enjoy matching standards of health care. Hospitals still under the control of religious orders were reorganized as public corporations to be governed by boards of trustees, who were elected to represent the interests of the communities they served.

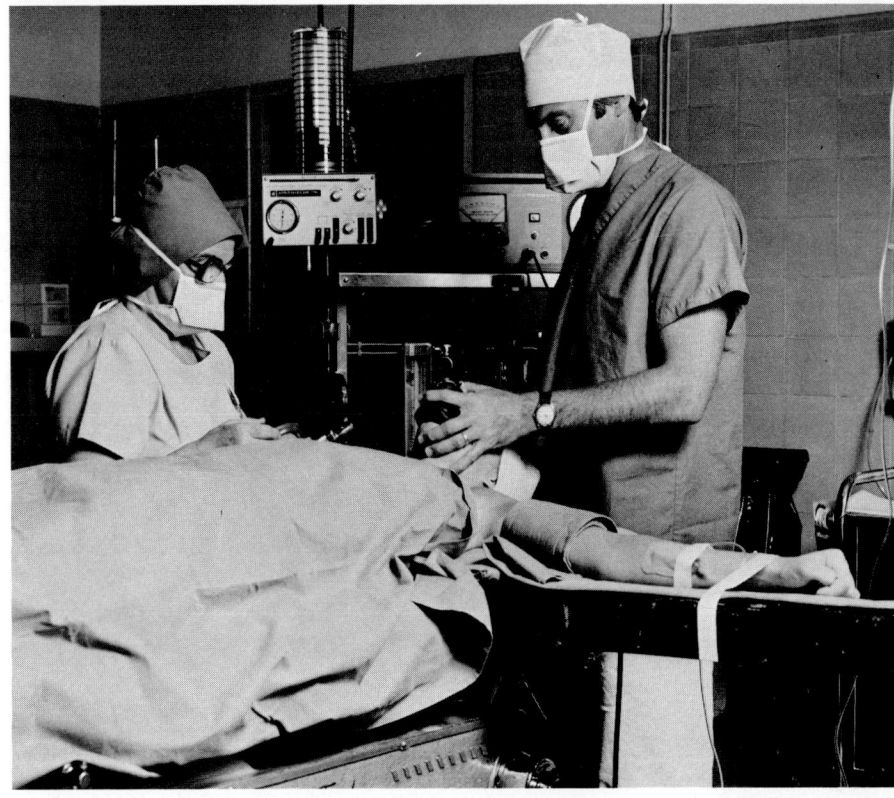

THE CHURCH

Quebec's Quiet Revolution followed patterns observed in other Catholic communities, particularly in Europe and South America. But in Quebec the changes were accomplished in a decade, while elsewhere evolution lasted a century or more.

The province is filled with reminders of the church's former pre-eminence. Schools and hospitals are surmounted by crosses. Fine churches and shrines occupy the focal points of towns and villages. Montreal and Quebec City street names refer to so many saints that motorists joke about riding in Paradise.

But these are souvenirs. The government's action of dislodging the church from health and education in the 1960s was accompanied by a cultural renaissance in which the church establishment — the 'ecclesiocracy' — played no part. New cultural leaders picked on the church as a scapegoat for the misfortunes of the whole population. They claimed that the church had en-

sured the survival of the French of Quebec not for their sake but for its own, to avoid being absorbed by the English. To achieve this the church had sided with the English to keep the French ignorant and poor, tied to parishes and family groups, and reproducing in abundance.

Such denouncements of the church quickly found favour among city-dwellers who had escaped the church's hold on country districts, and who now challenged its stern condemnation of contraceptives. At the same time leaders of the young were advocating Marxism as the antidote to Quebec's problems. The twin challenges took the ecclesiocracy by surprise.

In the parishes, particularly those in urban areas, church attendance swiftly declined. Many young priests, together with members of religious orders, entered salaried employment. The average age of parish priests rose to more than fifty, and the conservative attitudes held by many of these older priests did not help matters.

Aware of the significance of the social changes, progressive priests in

Montreal's Notre Dame has been described as the most beautiful church in North America.

Quebec adopted views radically different from the church's standard policies and drew curt censure from the Vatican. In the early 1970s, however, the Vatican itself reappraised the church's place in the world and proclaimed resolutions that ended 400 years of rigid control.

In the 1960s church leaders in Quebec had been torn between loyalty to the Vatican and the need to respond to the Quiet Revolution, and had solved the dilemma by maintaining a long silence. From this they slowly emerged during the 1970s, confining themselves to social and religious issues rather than political platforms.

On politics the church's stand was that there was nothing God-given about Canada's Confederation, and that it was certainly not immutable. On the other hand it was not the church's place to press for Quebec separatism or independence. Emphasis was on *survivance* — the survival of the Quebec people and their culture — as always.

Quebec's bishops and archbishops regularly convene to discuss church policy. Cardinal Maurice Roy, the Archbishop of Quebec (*front row centre*), is Roman Catholic Primate of Canada.

Younger priests continue to develop new roles for the church. One is the ecumenical movement, in which the Roman Catholic church seeks common ground with churches of other denominations and also with the Jewish community. Many priests and sisters are active within the ordinary work sphere.

There is evidence that the church has reinterpreted its role in Quebec so successfully that a strong religious revival is in progress. The Quiet Revolution was a major upset, but the church has recovered from it and has profited from the experience. In spite of the widespread abuse it was made to suffer, the church remains a major presence in Quebec as it was in the beginning.

The most significant shrine in Quebec is the replica of a tiny chapel (*far left*) built by shipwrecked Breton sailors at Ste. Anne de Beaupré. Nearby is the glorious Basilica of Sainte Anne, which is visited by tens of thousands of pilgrims each year.

The Bishops

The Archbishop of Quebec City is the province's primate and Canada's too. The office dates back to the appointment of Mgr. François Laval in 1674, at which time the Quebec see included all of North America north of Mexico, making it the world's largest. Today Quebec itself is divided into twenty dioceses, each being autonomous for its internal purposes.

A typical diocese is headed by a bishop and a vicar-general, and under them are two councils — the *conseil pastoral*, consisting of specialist clergy and laity and dealing with ecclesiastical policies, and the *conseil presbytéral*, consisting of priests of the diocese elected by their fellows and dealing with administration.

Each diocese is divided into parishes, grouped in pastoral zones to co-ordinate their efforts and implement common policies. Each is headed by a *curé* (priest). The Montreal region includes many non-francophone parishes, serving the English and Italian communities.

The dioceses are grouped in pastoral zones like the parishes, and the groups are centred on Quebec City, Montreal, Hull (Western Quebec), and Rimouski (Eastern Quebec). Dioceses act together in studying particular pastoral problems of the region.

In addition, all bishops are members of the Assembly of Bishops of Quebec. The Assembly is Quebec's church parliament, promoting unity in the pastory and making sure that all elements in the church work in concert. The Quebec Assembly belongs to the Canadian Assembly of Catholic Bishops, which considers problems that affect the national interest.

WORDS AND MUSIC

Largely a product of the Quiet Revolution, which heralded the return of French nationalism from about 1960, Quebec's folk *chanson* has become its most lasting memorial. It is the symbol of French Canada's renaissance.

The Quebeckers have always been singers. Early visitors to Canada delighted in the canoe songs by which voyageur paddlers paced themselves. Most were adapted from old French originals — notably *Alouette* — sometimes with heavy local connotations. In the early years of the twentieth century, however, Quebec fell prey to modern imports from France and the United States.

Then came Félix Leclerc, who in the 1950s travelled the province with simple songs celebrating the uniqueness of the Quebeckers. He sang of everyday life and of farmers, log-drivers, and lumberjacks, and encouraged those who heard him to take real pride in their French heritage and their culture.

Where Leclerc led, others followed. Gilles Vigneault returned to traditional melodies, but with provocative lyrics which reflected the political feelings and ambitions of the day. One by one the *chansonniers* became known to all Quebeckers, and they took on star stature — so much so that a sophisticated recording industry came into being around them.

Where English-speaking Canada refused to recognize local heroes (except sports stars), Quebec revelled in the *chansonniers*. Claude Léveillée, Jean-Pierre Ferland, Pauline Julien, Ginette Reno, Louise Forestier, Robert Charlebois, Diane Dufresne, and a score of others were added to the gallery.

Eventually even European French took notice, and the Quebec *chanson* went international. Meanwhile, the cultural revival spread to other spheres. The efforts of Raymond Lévesque established Quebec monologue as an art form. Other monologuists appeared, most notably Yvon Deschamps who soon became one of Canada's highest-paid entertainers.

Monologues and *chansons* took hold of Quebeckers' imagination, and were credited with helping to elect the Parti Québécois in 1976. The performers and their views were better known than the politicians, and it was the performers who had proclaimed most loudly that Quebec was for Quebeckers.

Their efforts mirrored parallel developments in literature. Before the Quiet Revolution, few Quebec novelists had been known to more than a tiny public — unless their work was adapted for radio or television, like Roger Lemelin's *Plouffe Family*. Then in the 1960s a new kind of writing appeared.

The first major breakthrough was a book by a teaching brother, Jean-Paul Desbiens, *The Impertinences of Brother Anonymous*. It was a satire on the educational system, and sparked fierce debate on social, religious, and academic conflicts. The book was a best seller, and opened the way for a stream of creative writing in prose and poetry.

Novelists like Gabrielle Roy, Anne Hébert, Roger Fournier, and Yves Thériault gained new prominence. Their books reflected the frustrations of Quebec society. So did those of newcomers like Hubert Aquin, Jacques Godbout, and Suzanne Paradis, while Marie-Claire Blais and Réjean Ducharme were accused of exaggerating the situation to make their points.

These Quebec novels have been well received in France and at home,

Five leading chansonniers come together for a concert series: (*from left*) **Claude Léveillée, Yvon Deschamps, Jean-Pierre Ferland, Gilles Vigneault, and Robert Charlebois.**

and are available in English translation. Several Quebec novelists have their work published in Paris rather than in Montreal. Interestingly, since the election of the Parti Québécois, several have forsaken tales of defeat and frustration and have turned, instead, to stories of conquest and success.

However, not all Quebec writing is in French. Many of Mordecai Richler's novels and short stories and Leonard Cohen's novels and poems (and English *chansons*) spring from their experience of Montreal. Hugh MacLennan of McGill University is one of the best-known novelists and essayists in Canada, and the playwright David Fennario has won great acclaim.

Turning again to music, Quebec has two professional symphony orchestras — the Montreal Symphony and the Quebec Symphony in Quebec City — and, in addition, the McGill Chamber Orchestra. There are choral groups throughout the province, another reminder that in Quebec 'everything begins and ends with a song.'

First broadcast in 1956, Radio-Canada's daily 'Bobino,' with Guy Sanche, is the world's longest-running children's television program.

The Montreal Symphony Orchestra plays regularly in the Place des Arts.

Marie-Claire Blais   **Anne Hébert**

Raymond Lévesque   **Félix Leclerc**

Pauline Julien   **Louise Forestier**

VISUAL ARTS

Tourists both in Old Montreal and Old Quebec are quickly attracted by artists they find working in the open air, in the Paris tradition. Some of the work exhibited is of reasonable quality and much is not, but tourists rely on their own tastes.

The open-air artists are the most obvious evidence of Quebec's continuing tradition of modern painting, which has been as much a symptom of cultural renaissance as progress elsewhere in the arts. It reaches back to the influence of William Brymner, director of classes at Montreal's Art Association at the turn of the century.

In 1900 Brymner stated: 'The real artist sees in a new light. We feel to be true that which he shows us, though we have never thought of it before in that way.' Quick to demonstrate his perceptions were three landscape painters working in Quebec independently — James Wilson Morrice, Maurice Cullen, and Marc-Aurèle Suzor-Coté.

These three men and younger contemporaries like Clarence Gagnon were Canada's first impressionists. Their work was continued by Alfred Pellan, 'Quebec's Picasso,' who returned to Quebec during World War II after many years spent in France. First he exhibited with Toronto's Canadian Group of Painters, then later on his own.

Pellan's sudden prominence urged other artists working in Quebec to band together more closely. They came to be called *Les Peintures Automatistes*. Like Pellan they were impressionistic, but they were also a recognizable school in themselves, and were associated with far-reaching social and political views based on ideals of Quebec independence.

The *Automatistes* were centred on Paul-Emile Borduas, a fiery theorist who in 1948 drafted *Le Refus Global*, which was later endorsed by others of the group. This was a social and political manifesto, demanding unified cultural action and pledging that 'we shall follow joyfully our violent fight for liberation.'

Members of the group gathered strength and influence in the 1950s. Besides Borduas, they included Léon Bellefleur and Jean-Paul Riopelle, who

Leon Bellefleur's *Châtiment de Méduse*, **1954, oil on canvas.**

Saint-Jean-Port-Joli, on the south bank of the St. Lawrence, is famous for wood sculpture. **It is the home of the scupltors' school run by Médard Bourgault.**

78

Outdoor portrait artists provide an exotic touch in both Montreal and Quebec City.

later resided in France, and Marcelle Ferron and Fernand Leduc. Separate from them was Jean-Paul Lemieux, whose impressionistic style has special appeal to Quebeckers.

A second school emerged during the later 1950s. This was *Les Plasticiens*, who painted to strict geometric concepts then in vogue in New York. Its early proponents were not well received, but the hard-edged style gained strength through the work of Guido Molinari of Montreal during the 1960s.

Recent years have seen a steady flowering of artistic life in Quebec, not least a 'realist' school pioneered during the 1960s whose work is characterized by a painstaking devotion to detail. Graphic art flourished in the early 1970s but as the decade advanced individual artists used a great variety of styles.

In the field of sculpture, Quebec is famous for woodcarving. Its roots go back to the origins of New France, when Bishop Laval brought artisans from Europe to carve embellishments on church property. The skills have been kept alive, particularly in the sculptors' school run by Médard Bourgault in Saint-Jean-Port-Joli. However, most woodcarving is now regarded as the province of artisans rather than of artists, and the mainstream has passed it by.

In stone, academic sculptors of the nineteenth century, like Napoleon Bourassa, Anatole Parthenais, and Philippe Hébert, left fine examples of their work, including statues throughout Montreal and Quebec City.

The great emergence of modern sculpture came in the 1930s — yet another manifestation of cultural renaissance. Artists were enabled to study new materials and fresh techniques, and were encouraged to develop works of art for public display. Not all have been well received, and many of Quebec's modern sculptures have been damaged by vandals.

One field of sculpture which has gained rapidly in popularity has been Inuit carving from Northern Quebec, distributed through co-operatives run by the Inuit themselves. These works, of soapstone, walrus tusks, caribou antlers, and such materials, represent arctic animals, legendary and mythical beings, and family and hunting scenes.

Alfred Pellan's *Sous-terre*, **1938, oil on canvas.**

STAGE AND FILM

The performing arts in Quebec have developed along much the same lines as literature and painting. Traditions are deep-rooted, but only in recent times has real Québécois expression come to the fore.

This has been due not so much to performers as to their material. Playwrights like Marcel Dubé, Françoise Loranger, and Gratien Gélinas have given Quebec much to think about. So has Jacques Languirand, whose work is stark and perhaps obscure. The catchy *joual* street dialect of Michel Tremblay's plays remind Montrealers and other Quebeckers of their deep roots.

The advances have been paced by Canada's National Theatre School in Montreal, which offers parallel courses for French-speaking and English-speaking actors and a co-lingual production course. The English acting course is significantly more conservative than the French. For example, where English actors are given fencing lessons to equip them for Shakespeare, the French section actively seeks brand new works from Quebec playwrights, specially written for the school's productions. These

plays and others — six major and six minor productions each year — are staged in the school's own theatre.

Students of the school are drawn from all over Canada and are selected on the basis of talent alone. Inevitably most of the francophone actors are drawn from Quebec. Most of those who finish the course are able to earn a livelihood within the profession, whether in stage or film work, or in advertising.

Some of the francophone actors gravitate to the various professional companies in Montreal — notably the Théâtre du Nouveau Monde, Le Rideau-Vert, La Nouvelle Compagnie Théâtrale, and Le Théâtre de Quat'Sous. Among theatres in which they perform are Montreal's Place des Arts and Quebec City's Grand Théâtre de Québec.

However, opportunities in the professional companies are limited, and many young actors have formed their own troupes. These tour the province and make forays beyond its boundaries, staging experimental and avant-garde pieces with their roots in Quebec. Others join in summer seasons, when plays are staged throughout the province.

The Opéra du Québec stages *Samson et Dalila* **in the Grande Théâtre de Québec, Quebec City.**

As in the world of theatre, Quebec has made considerable strides in opera and dance. The Opéra du Québec founded in 1971 succeeded a series of earlier ventures. The 1960s saw a revival of interest in folk dancing and eventually the emergence of troupes like Les Gens de Mon Pays and Les Farandoles.

As regards classical dancing, Les Grands Ballets Canadiens are based in Montreal. The troupe was formed in the 1950s and tours Canada and the United States. The Entre-Six group presents both classical and modern ballet, and a number of modern dance troupes have turned professional, including the Groupe de la Place Royale.

Not far removed from the theatre world is Quebec's film industry. Canada's first known film was shot in Quebec City in 1897, as British engineers erected the monument to Wolfe and Montcalm. In the years that followed a variety of films were produced, few of which are of any interest today.

In 1939, however, the Canadian government established the National Film Board to initiate and promote film production and distribution in the na-

A student production of Jean Genet's *The Balcony*, by the National Theatre School of Canada in Montreal.

The National Film Board of Canada has become famous for the animated films of Norman McLaren, which have won many international awards.

tional interest, and particularly to interpret Canada to Canadians and to other nations. World War II established the NFB as a potent force in the international film world.

The NFB was co-lingual, and its French-medium division provided perfect opportunities for the nascent Quebec film industry. This was reinforced in 1956 when the NFB's operational headquarters were moved from Ottawa to Montreal. Quebec directors like Claude Jutra, Michel Brault, and Gilles Carle had their start with the NFB.

The advent of French television in 1952 dealt a hard blow to the film industry, but with the Quiet Revolution, independent film-makers came to prominence. At first they worked in 'international' French, hoping for an export market, but later some resorted to true Quebec *joual*, as did contemporary playwrights.

In the 1970s the Quebec film industry has had much critical success, in spite of earlier flirtations with the box office through a series of sex movies in the later 1960s. Its reputation was fully restored when Brault's *Les Ordres*, about the 1970 FLQ crisis, won him the award for best director at the 1976 Cannes film festival.

Gilles Carle   Michel Brault

Claude Jutra   Jean Paul LeFebvre

Four of the most prominent Québécois film directors, all of whom had their start with the National Film Board.

HOCKEY

Most Canadians agree that the national sport is hockey rather than lacrosse. Quebeckers lay special claim to hockey. Some would say that the game — particularly as played by the Montreal Canadiens — helped keep Quebeckers' nationalism alive during dark days.

Where hockey originated is a moot point. Kingston, Halifax, and Montreal all have their proponents, and concrete records go back at least to 1855. But what is certain is that in 1875 students of McGill University devised the McGill Rules of competition, which were soon adopted by teams throughout Eastern Canada.

In the years that followed, leagues were formed. By 1893 the sport was so well established that the governor-general, Lord Stanley, donated a sterling-silver trophy to be awarded annually to the outstanding team. Originally all teams were amateur, but the rules did not exclude professionals and these came to dominate the competition.

Early competitions featured several teams from Montreal. A club held the trophy until beaten by a challenger, and the right to challenge was determined in a series of play-offs. The Montreal Canadiens won the trophy for the first time in the 1915–16 competition, a year before the formation of Canada's National Hockey League.

In its first season the league consisted of only three teams — the Canadiens, the Ottawa Senators, and the Toronto Arenas. Slowly its membership expanded to include teams from the United States, until by 1929 it included ten. From this high point the number was reduced as teams dropped out, until only six were left — the Canadiens, the Toronto Maple Leafs, and teams from New York, Chicago, Boston, and Detroit. Some years later the league expanded again, but it was in those golden years that Quebec hockey fervour concentrated on the Canadiens and on their home arena, the Montreal Forum. In

The Canadiens' defence stave off an attack by the New York Rangers. For home games in the Forum the Canadiens wear white uniforms; for away games they wear their famous red.

The Quebec Nordiques were formed in 1972 to play in the World Hockey Association. They won that league's Avco Cup in 1976–1977. Here they meet the Indianapolis Racers.

82

retrospect it appears that francophone Quebeckers (or at least Montrealers) relieved the frustrations they experienced at the hands of the English establishment and the church at the Forum.

Certainly Canadien heroes assumed almost divine status, and none more convincingly than Maurice 'Rocket' Richard, who through his determined play revolutionized the game. When Richard was suspended by the league before the Stanley Cup play-offs of 1955, the Forum crowd took to the streets of Montreal in an orgy of destruction.

The hockey riot marked the first time that Quebec had made world headlines, and perhaps the eruption from the Forum was the beginning of the (not-so-quiet) revolution which caused such upheavals in the 1960s. From that point Quebec nationalism could not be contained.

It might be superficial to suggest that the fortunes of Quebec mirror those of the Canadiens, or vice versa, but that appears to be the case, and inevitably that is what many Quebeckers feel. A triumph for the team is a triumph for French Canada, and its disgrace is Quebec's shame.

During winter, hockey is played wherever there is ice, and it remains an ambition for each young hockey player in Quebec to wear a Canadiens shirt. Many players find their way to professional teams — if not to the Canadiens, then perhaps to the Quebec Nordiques, formed in 1972 and supported by a keen following in Quebec City. Others play elsewhere in Canada and the United States.

But the chief focus is always the Forum, where Canadiens fans must surely be the world's champion hockey connoisseurs. So they should be, after decades of observing players like Maurice Richard, Jean Beliveau, who captained the team in its golden years, and the more recent hero, Guy Lafleur.

A dangerous moment for the Canadiens as their goalkeeper sprawls full length on the ice, with the Philadelphia Flyers attacking.

Stanley Cup

Since the hockey riot of 1955, the Montreal Canadiens have dominated the Stanley Cup competition, in spite of the steady expansion of the National Hockey League to a high of eighteen teams in 1974. All are in the United States except the Canadiens, the Maple Leafs, and the Vancouver Canucks.

Winners since 1955–1956 are as follows:

1955–1956 Montreal Canadiens	1966–1967 Toronto Maple Leafs
1956–1957 Montreal Canadiens	1967–1968 Montreal Canadiens
1957–1958 Montreal Canadiens	1968–1969 Montreal Canadiens
1958–1959 Montreal Canadiens	1969–1970 Boston Bruins
1959–1960 Montreal Canadiens	1970–1971 Montreal Canadiens
1960–1961 Chicago Black Hawks	1971–1972 Boston Bruins
1961–1962 Toronto Maple Leafs	1972–1973 Montreal Canadiens
1962–1963 Toronto Maple Leafs	1973–1974 Philadelphia Flyers
1963–1964 Toronto Maple Leafs	1974–1975 Philadelphia Flyers
1964–1965 Montreal Canadiens	1975–1976 Montreal Canadiens
1965–1966 Montreal Canadiens	1976–1977 Montreal Canadiens

RECREATION

Besides establishing hockey rules, students of McGill University are credited with promoting Canadian Rugby Football. In the 1870s they accepted a challenge to play Harvard University, and so introduced the game to the United States.

In that country, college football has gone on to become the number one spectator sport. In Canada, however, chief focus is on professional teams within the Canadian Football League. One of the best is the Montreal Alouettes, which carries a high profile in the annual Grey Cup competition.

Besides the Alouettes, Montreal supports its Canadiens hockey team and also the baseball professionals, the Montreal Expos. Both the Expos and the Alouettes play in the Olympic stadium. The baseball team was founded in 1969 and plays in the National League, Canada's only major league baseball franchise apart from the Toronto Blue Jays.

But most sport in Quebec is amateur. It received a considerable boost from the 1976 Olympic Games held in Montreal, which showed young Quebeckers the high standard expected in sports that were familiar and many that were not. Especially enlightening were the canoe events, based on a sport largely originated in Quebec.

At a more modest level, each year the province runs the Quebec Games, which are split into winter and summer sections like the Olympics and the Canada Games. Both sections are organized every year, and involve not only finals but a range of preliminary

Like a herd of caribou on the move, cross-country skiers set out on a day's excursion.

regional elimination contests, which involve nearly 100 000 Quebeckers.

The summer games are primarily track and field, though other sports are being added, and the winter games include such events as skiing and skating. Besides the games there are many other important events, like the international long-distance swim classic across Lac St. Jean. The distance involved is just short of 33 km, from Peribonka to Roberval, and each year the event attracts strong competition from many countries (with Canadians more than holding their own) and tens of thousands of spectators. The quality of performance depends largely on the weather and the state of the water.

Another international race is the annual Tour de la Nouvelle France, a cycling marathon like the famous Tour de France in Europe. The event covers some 800 km, starting and finishing in Montreal and taking in most of southern Quebec's chief cities along a generally flat course.

With Quebec snowbound for half the year, it is no surprise that winter sports flourish throughout the province. The most basic are snowshoeing for fun (though some race is earnest) and ice fishing (particularly at the annual ice fishing festival held at Le Perade near Trois Rivières).

There are four main ski areas in Quebec, all well up to international standards. The longest-established is the Laurentians range north of Montreal, including the famous Mont Tremblant, which is the best-known ski resort in Eastern Canada. North of Hull are the resorts in the Outaouais — dubbed 'Ski-O' by English-speakers.

Ski East is located in the Eastern Townships, including five ski locations notable for their spectacular scenery and inns with impressive cuisine. The fourth area is north and east of Quebec City. Its major attraction is Mont Ste. Anne, just a metre or two short of qualifying as an Olympic and World Cup downhill mountain.

Besides these downhill resorts, all Quebec provides fine opportunities for the cross-country skier. When the first snow falls each year, some Canadians are saddened because it emphasizes that fall is over. Many Quebeckers, on the other hand, are ecstatic that winter has begun.

The annual long-distance swimming race across Lac St. Jean has become an international event.

Snowshoes were adopted by early settlers from local Indians, and today provide one of Quebec's favourite winter recreations.

Young cyclists take to the road in the heat of summer.

where the accent is generally on French or, at any rate, 'international' cuisine. Instead the best regional dishes are found at home, and particularly in the country. But there is rising interest in local styles even in restaurants, especially among tourists.

Tourism is one of the province's top money-earners, and at the regional level it is often crucial. Its importance led the Quebec government to set up North America's (and probably the world's) most sophisticated tourism and hotel school, which came into being in Montreal in 1968.

The institute sprang from cooking courses offered in a government trade school, and cuisine has remained an essential part of its curriculum. Its central theme is traditional French style, the basis of international cuisine. In addition there is instruction in Italian and Chinese cooking, and also in Quebec regional style.

Restaurant cuisine in Quebec is centred on the French tradition, though there is increasing interest in Quebec specialties.

Quebec produces no wine of its own, but imports the best wines from France and other countries.

FOOD AND WINE

A beneficial result of Quebeckers' new confidence in themselves is a resurgence of regional cuisine. It is easy to trace close links between some Quebec specialties and their direct forebears in western France, but many are of purely local origin.

Traditional Quebec cuisine tends to be a little heavy to North American taste — a reflection of early arrivals' need for energy-rich foods to carry them through the winter. The predominance of flour and meat in stews, fricassees, pies, roasts, and *gibelottes* makes for hearty eating.

Prime examples of versions of French originals are *tourtière* (chopped pork or veal pie) and *six-pâtes* (a deep pot-pie made of partridge, hare, quail, potatoes, and lard or bacon flavoured with cloves). Others are *ragoût de boulettes et de pattes de cochon* (meat-balls and pig's feet stew) and *soupe à la gourgane* made with broad beans.

Of course, French-Canadian pea soup (made with white beans) is the most famous of Quebec specialties and has given rise to a whole folklore of its own. Just as distinctive are the many sweets made with maple syrup — ideas borrowed from the Indian tribes who first tapped the sweet liquid. These include sugar pie, eggs cooked in boiling maple syrup and served hot or cold, *tarte à la ferouche* (dried raisins and maple syrup), and *tourquettes* (made by pouring boiling maple syrup from vats on to snow where it congeals). And then there are the many cheeses made in Quebec — among them the famous cheese made by the Trappist monks of Oka.

As yet Quebec cuisine has made little impression on better restaurants,

High standards of cuisine mean that Montrealers are among North America's most discriminating gourmets.

The school offers courses at high school and CEGEP level and is quickly developing a university level too. Its chief advantage is that it combines North American business know-how with European practical style, and it has assembled a greater concentration of teaching capacity than any other hotel school in the world.

One of its most unexpected features is a forty-room hotel, operated as part of the school. It is run by the students themselves, working in kitchens, restaurants, bars, rooms, or behind the reception counter. Graduates from the school are raising hotel and catering standards throughout Quebec.

An important part of the school curriculum is wine science, or oenology. As with food, the school concentrates on French traditions, though appreciation of all wines is encouraged. Quebec makes no wine of its own (unless one counts blueberry wine, now made north of the St. Lawrence) but it imports a rich variety from France.

It is no accident that the school is located in Montreal, which has an assortment of restaurants equalled nowhere else in North America except in New York City. That (and its atmosphere) is what makes Montreal a magnet for tourists. Quebec City has many fine restaurants too, and others are scattered throughout the province.

The Quebec government has a rating system for restaurants operating in hotels, as it has for the hotels themselves, reflecting services provided and the quality of those services. But it deliberately avoids trying to rate independent restaurants, because their standards are bound to fluctuate.

Early Quebeckers adapted traditional cooking styles from France to the food supplies they discovered in the New World, and the principle still applies. Here a fisherman displays a fine Arctic char caught in Northern Quebec.

THE OUTDOORS

Montreal and Quebec City are prime attractions to Quebeckers and visitors alike. But while the Quebeckers know that the province has a great deal more to offer, many outsiders never venture beyond the cities. This is a pity, for it means that they miss the real strength of Quebec — the ongoing country traditions that sustained Quebec habitants through the difficult years of 'foreign' occupation. Even many city-dwellers are acutely conscious of their rural past, and remain staunchly loyal to a particular region.

Throughout the St. Lawrence valley and as far as the tip of the Gaspé Peninsula, farms and villages remain to show how the habitants have always lived. Ancient churches and manor-houses in the seigneuries date back to the seventeenth century. All through the year local folk festivals keep old skills and achievements alive.

But just as important as this cultural heritage is the Quebec outdoors, the other major element in the province's tradition. For Quebeckers the year's seasons are punctuated by outdoor activities — snowshoeing and skiing in winter, maple syrup tapping in spring, canoeing and hunting in summer, and fishing in the fall.

Many of these activities take place in the various provincial parks established by the government to conserve some of Quebec's best features. Several were originally set aside for wildlife conservation, others specifically for recreation, and a few for particular cultural pursuits. They include a series of attractive parks north of the St. Lawrence which are readily accessible from the major cities. These are: Papineau–Labelle north of Hull, Mont Tremblant and Joliette north of Montreal, Mastigouche and Saint-Maurice north of Trois Rivières, and Portneuf and the great Laurentides Park less than 100 km from Quebec City.

Most of the parks offer varied terrain of forested hills and valleys and plenty of water in the way of lakes and rivers. All have excellent fishing, most are open all year (for skidooing in winter), and some have hunting for small game. The Laurentides' great pride is its herd of caribou, re-established there in 1969.

The Laurentides Park was set aside as early as 1895 to prevent warring between Montagnais Indians, who hunted there, with rival Hurons from the south. The idea was to 'preserve the primitive forest, the fish, and the game, to maintain a constant reserve of water, and to encourage the study and cultivation of forest vegetation.'

At 9752 km² the park is an enormous expanse, but it is not the largest. La Vérendrye Park north of Hull (13 615 km²) was set aside in 1939; Chibougamau (11 025 km²), set up in 1946 north-west of Lac St. Jean, is a fishing paradise; its neighbour, Mistassini (24 529 km²), is a beaver reserve. There is one other large provincial park — Port Cartier–Sept-Iles in the east, intended as another vast beaver reserve. It assures conservation of the species and permits trapping for the benefit of local Indians. All the large parks offer limited accommodation, but are really best suited to wilderness camping.

Smaller and more accessible parks have been established south of the St. Lawrence — Gaspésie, Matane, Dunière, Rimouski in the Gaspé, and others even smaller. Gaspésie has the last herd of caribou south of the Gulf, and Matami and Dunière hold Canada's highest concentration of moose.

There is fine fishing (and canoeing) throughout the province, and Quebeckers take full advantage of it — especially up the salmon rivers of the Gulf coast and along the abundant trout streams. Complex regulations surround hunting in the province, based on open season quotas designed to conserve the natural balance.

Disturbed by an airplane, caribou stampede across the snow of Ungava in the far north of Quebec.

Canoe campers set out on the next leg of their journey in the huge Parc de la Vérendrye in western Quebec.

Quebec has a considerable population of black bears, but nobody knows exactly how many.

Matami and Dunière provincial parks in the Gaspé hold Canada's highest concentration of moose.

INDIANS AND INUIT

The James Bay development scheme announced in 1971 provoked strong reaction among native peoples, who believed they would be adversely affected. In 1973 a Superior Court judge backed the Quebec Cree by approving a permanent injunction against the scheme.

The judgement was overturned in the Quebec Court of Appeal. Rather than take the matter further, the native peoples — not Cree alone, but also the Inuit of the north — negotiated a settlement in which they agreed to abandon their aboriginal claims to the whole of New Quebec (northern Quebec) in exchange for substantial rights and payments.

The settlement affects some 6500 Cree living in the south-west of New Quebec, and about 4500 Inuit living in thirteen scattered settlements on the Hudson Bay coast, along Hudson Strait, and around Ungava Bay. They have been awarded a cash payment of $225 million spread over twenty years.

In addition they have been granted rights and privileges over land. These include exclusive hunting, fishing, and trapping rights around local communities in areas carefully selected and demarcated. The provincial government assumes possession of mineral and sub-surface rights, but may not develop them without native approval.

Apart from these guaranteed lands, Cree and Inuit have been promised extensive areas where again they enjoy exclusive hunting, fishing, and trapping. But in this case they have no special rights to occupancy, and the provincial government may develop the land. However, in that event it is obliged to provide replacement lands elsewhere.

The readiness of the Cree and Inuit to surrender their aboriginal rights was criticized by native groups elsewhere in Canada. Those involved insist that if they had not come to terms, they might have found themselves without rights, land, money, or written undertakings from the provincial or federal governments.

Other smaller groups may have claims in New Quebec. The provincial government has committed itself to determine what is due to them and to

Fort Chimo, Quebec's leading Inuit community, was founded in 1828 as a Hudson's Bay Company trading post. It is located on the Koksoak river, which runs into Ungava Bay.

Northern Quebec is thinly populated. The Cree nation, the largest group that lives there, was largely responsible for the negotiation of the James Bay Agreement. ▼

Following an onslaught by marauding Iroquois in 1649, Hurons of Western Ontario sought the protection of the French colonists at Quebec. Their descendants remain in the Village des Hurons near Quebec City, where they hand-make canoes (shown here) and snowshoes.

Young Inuit at Fort Chimo. One in four of Canadian Inuit lives in Quebec.

take action accordingly. They include the Naskapis — Indians of the northern interior who still live by hunting and trapping — and perhaps the Montagnais of the south-east.

But it is the Cree who are being affected most by the development of James Bay, at least in the short term. Already they have profited from employment opportunities offered in construction activities, and it may be expected that they will utilize their share of the cash payments to develop their society.

Certainly the Inuit plan to invest their money in new industries to provide themselves with future employment, though they have not yet decided how. In their case, the chief problem is the inaccessibility of their communities except by air and for a short season each year by sea.

In numbers the Inuit of Quebec seem few — though even so, they account for one in four of all Inuit in Canada. But they have preserved more Inuit traditions and skills than their counterparts in the Northwest Territories, and seem determined not to lose them as they upgrade their settlements along the rugged coasts. One feature of the provincial government's plans for them is the creation of an enormous regional authority to govern the whole of the area north of the 55th parallel, to be run by Inuit themselves. The area's administrative and chief distribution centre is Fort Chimo, set on a river running into Ungava Bay.

Fort Chimo was first established as a trading post in 1828, when New Quebec was still part of Rupert's Land and the preserve of the Hudson's Bay Company. Fort George, the principal settlement on the James Bay coast and now occupied chiefly by Cree, was a post established in 1884. Both dealt principally with Naskapi trappers.

All these peoples have traditionally relied on hunting, trapping, and fishing to provide not only food but all the necessities of life. Their greatest debt is to the caribou. But the spread of civilization is bringing profound changes to their existence, not all welcome. They need every encouragement as they strive to combine the best of the new with the best of the old.

THE ISLANDS

Within Quebec's borders are many beautiful islands with fascinating characteristics. They include the Ile d'Orléans in the St. Lawrence river, and Anticosti and the Magdalen Islands in the Gulf of St. Lawrence.

The Ile d'Orléans was discovered by Jacques Cartier on his second voyage. He named it the Isle of Bacchus because of the profusion of wild grapes he found growing there. The island is about 34 km long and 9 km wide, and it is a few kilometres downstream of Quebec City. It played a prominent part in Wolf's siege of 1759.

Today the island can be reached by bridge from the St. Lawrence's north shore, and it delights even visiting Quebeckers, because the first impressions are that little has changed since the eighteenth century. Buildings are intact, and the island is still divided into a handful of parishes grouped around their churches. The island is splendidly fertile, and farmers grow fruit and vegetables. In summer these are sold from stands along the roads, and apples, strawberries, and plums are especially popular. In summer the Gosselin mill near St. Laurent and an ancient barn at St. Pierre are used as arts centres, and they present annual festivals.

The Ile d'Orléans has developed into a tourist attraction, but Anticosti Island in the Gulf retains its accustomed low profile. It also was discovered by Jacques Cartier, who in 1535 named it Ile de l'Assomption. Later travellers preferred its Indian name, *Naticousti*, derived from a term meaning 'where bears are hunted.'

Anticosti is about 200 km long, and at its maximum nearly 50 km wide. It was granted to the explorer Louis Jolliet of Quebec City in 1680, and held by his family until after the British conquest of 1760, when it was annexed to Newfoundland. In 1774 it was returned to Canada, but no effort to colonize it was made until 1874. The first colonists were from Newfoundland, but their attempt failed, as did a second attempt in 1884. Then the island was sold to the French chocolate manufacturer Henri Menier,

The little port of Cap-aux-Meules is the biggest community in the Magdalen Islands.

Descendants of deer released on Anticosti in the nineteenth century make it a hunter's paradise.

who built a village and a château and poured money into developing the island's resources. In 1926 the island was sold to a group of pulp and paper companies.

Now it belongs to the provincial government. It is a hunter's and fisherman's paradise, containing rich salmon and trout streams and abundant deer, descended from stock introduced by Menier. However, as yet only limited facilities have been installed, and Anticosti is visited by only a handful of outsiders each year.

Anticosti is difficult to reach, but it is not as remote as the sixteen Magdalen Islands used to be. Far out in the Gulf, they were the last resort of fugitives from the Maritime provinces and from Quebec. Today these islands are accessible both by air and by ferry from Prince Edward Island and the northern shore of the Gulf, but they remain unspoiled.

The Magdalen Islands are set in a curve about 95 km long, and some are linked by sandbars and lagoons. Most are low-lying, though there is high ground too, since they are part of the Appalachian system. The islands, like so many others, were discovered by Jacques Cartier in 1534, and were explored by Champlain in 1603. Sealing and fishing are the Magdalens' traditional industries, particularly fishing for lobster, herring, and mackerel. Recently, however, the islands' exceptional beaches and unusual atmosphere have attracted a strong flow of tourists from the mainland. Half the 10 000-odd population lives on Cap-aux-Meules.

There are many other islands and island groups near Quebec, particularly along the Hudson Strait and within Hudson Bay. Inuit inhabitants of these northern islands have close connections with their cousins in New Quebec. However, as arrangements stand, the islands fall within the Northwest Territories.

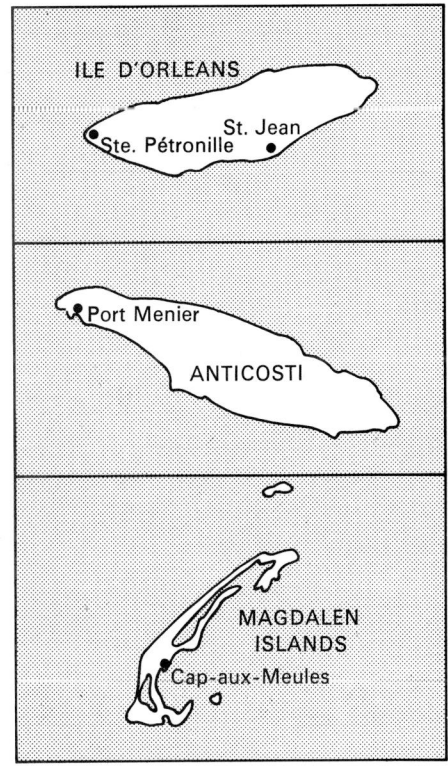

(Maps differ in scale.)

Quebec's southern islands are (*from top*) **the Ile d'Orléans, near Quebec City, Anticosti, in the Gulf of St. Lawrence, and the Magdalen Islands, east of the Gaspé.**

Old skills have been passed on from generation to generation on the Ile d'Orléans near Quebec City. The island's *artisanat* **is a flourishing tourist attraction.**

A high point of the Quebec carnival is canoe racing across the frozen St. Lawrence.

Revellers at Chicoutimi carnival enjoy a local variety of *tourtière*, or meat pie.

CARNIVAL

Quebeckers enliven the depths of winter by celebrating it. Several communities organize winter carnivals, and one of the most successful is Chicoutimi's. Each year townsfolk recreate the atmosphere of a century ago.

Most famous, however, and a drawing card for visitors from all over the province, is the great carnival of Quebec City each February. Ruled for ten days by the Carnival *Bonhomme* — a giant snowman — Quebeckers enjoy organized activities and spontaneous encounters with friends and strangers alike.

The Quebec Carnival includes two spectacular night parades, followed by all-night dancing. But every night there is something of interest, and every day too. Favourite events are paddling races across the frozen St. Lawrence, and snow sculpture contests involving international teams.

The ingredients remain much the same from carnival to carnival. Many veteran revellers resort to a narrow street in the lower city. Its residents line the sidewalks with grotesque snow sculptures, and throngs of happy Quebeckers parade among them day and night.

Night parades at Quebec's winter carnival are graced by seven carnival princesses, representing the seven local regions.

Photograph Credits

Agriculture Canada: p. 26 top, p. 27 bottom; *Alcan*: p. 11 bottom right; *Les Archives du Québec*: p. 11 bottom right, p. 13 bottom left, p. 15 bottom right and centre, p. 17 top right and bottom right, p. 21 bottom right and left, p. 65 centre right and left, and bottom right and left; *Asbestos Corp.*: p. 38, p. 39 top; *L'Assemblée nationale*: (Les Photographes Kedl Ltée.) p. 66, p. 67 top; *Canada Dept. of Indian & Northern Affairs*: p. 91 top; *Canadair*: p. 32 top and bottom; *Canadian Industries Ltd.*: p. 28, p. 48, p. 49 bottom right, (Pierre Wibaut) p. 49 top; *Canadian International Paper*: p. 31 top and bottom left; *Celanese Canada*: p. 47 centre; *Cinemathèque Québécoise*: p. 81 bottom first row left and right, bottom second row left and right; *City of Montreal*: p. 58 bottom, p. 59 bottom, p. 60, p. 61 top, centre, and bottom, p. 77 bottom left, p. 79 top, p. 83, p. 86 top, p. 87 top; *Humphry Clinker*: p. 3, p. 13 bottom right, p. 15 bottom left, p. 46, p. 47 top, p. 62 top and bottom, p. 63 top and bottom, p. 67 bottom, p. 68 top and bottom, p. 69 bottom left, p. 75 top, p. 82 top and bottom; *Consolidated-Bathurst*: p. 34, (George Hunter) p. 35 top and bottom; *Dominion Textiles*: p. 47 bottom; *Editeur officiel du Québec*: p. 17 bottom left, p. 20 top, p. 21 top, p. 44 bottom, p. 64, p. 65 top; *Editions du Seuil Ltée.*: p. 77 top right; *Hydro-Quebec*: p. 50 top and bottom, p. 51 top; *Institut de Tourisme et d'Hotellerie du Québec*: p. 86 bottom; *Inventaire des Biens Culturels du Québec*: p. 11 bottom left; *Iron Ore Co. of Canada*: p. 22 top, p. 41 bottom right, p. 53 centre; *James Bay Development Corp.*: p. 4 top, p. 30 top, p. 87 bottom, p. 90 bottom, (Leo Henrichon) p. 7 bottom left; *James Bay Energy Corp*: p. 23 top; *Kebec-Disc*: p. 76; *Le Ministère de l'Agriculture*: p. 25 bottom, p. 27 top, p. 29 centre and bottom; *Le Ministère de l'Education*: p. 70 bottom, p. 71; *Le Ministère des Richesses Naturelles*: p. 55 bottom, p. 90 top, p. 91 bottom; *Le Ministère du Tourisme, de la Chasse et de la Pêche*: p. 5, p. 6 top and bottom, p. 19 top, p. 22 bottom, p. 24 top and bottom, p. 25 top, p. 26 bottom, p. 29 top, p. 31 top, p. 33 bottom, p. 36 top and bottom, p. 37 top and bottom, p. 39 bottom, p. 45 bottom, p. 58 top, p. 62 bottom, p. 74, p. 75 bottom, p. 78 bottom, p. 80, p. 84, p. 85 top, centre, and bottom, p. 88, p. 89 top, bottom right and left, p. 92 top and bottom, p. 93, p. 94 top, centre, and bottom; *Mirabel Airport*: p. 54 top; *Musée de l'Art Contemporain*: p. 78 top, p. 79 bottom; *Musée du Québec*: p. 4 bottom, p. 10 top right and left, bottom, p. 15 top, p. 19 bottom right and left; *National Film Board of Canada*: p. 81 bottom left; *The National Theatre School of Canada*: (Daniel Kieffer) p. 81 top; *Noranda Mines*: p. 40 bottom, (Feature Four Ltd.) p. 40 top, p. 42, p. 43 top; *Northern Telecom*: p. 56, p. 57 top, (Graetz Bros. Ltd.) p. 58 top; *Office du film du Québec*: p. 77 top centre; *Port of Montreal*: (Armour Landry) p. 52; *Québec-Cartier Mining*: p. 41 bottom left, p. 53 top; *Quebec Police*: p. 69 bottom right; *Radio-Canada*: p. 57 bottom left, p. 77 second row left and right, and third row right, (Jean-Pierre Karsenty) p. 77 third row left, (André Le Coz) p. 77 top row left, (Studio Lausanne Inc.) p. 57 bottom right; *Royal Victoria Hospital*: p. 72 top and bottom, p. 73 top and bottom; *Sidbec-Dosco*: (Audio Vidéothèque) p. 44 top, p. 45 top; *St. Lawrence Seaway Authority*: p. 53 bottom right; *Transport Canada*: p. 54 bottom, p. 55 top; *Union Carbide*: (Ron Vickers Ltd.) p. 49 bottom left; *Université Laval*: (Gérard Roger) p. 70 top.

Acknowledgments

We wish to thank the following individuals, corporations, departments, and organizations for their assistance and for making material from their collections available:

Agriculture Canada
Air Canada
Alcan Smelters and Chemicals
Archives du Québec
Asbestos Corporation Limited
Assemblée des Evêques du Québec
Assemblée Nationale du Québec
Association des Mines d'Amiante du Québec
Association des Mines de Metaux du Québec
Bar of Montreal
Leon Bellefleur
Bombardier Ltée
Lucien Campeau
Canadair
Canadian Industries Limited
Canadian International Paper Company
Canadian Johns-Manville Company, Limited
Canadian National
Canadian Pulp and Paper Association
Canadian Textiles Institute
Claude Castonguay
Celanese Canada
Cinemathèque Québécoise
City of Quebec
Consolidated Bathurst Limited
Couvent des Ursulines, Québec
Gérard Dion
Direction Général du Nouveau Québec
Dominion Textiles
Dupont of Canada
Environment Canada

Freedman Clothing
Geological Survey of Canada
Conrad Godin
Hydro–Québec
Institut de Tourisme et d'Hôtellerie
Iron Ore Company of Canada
James Bay Development Corporation
James Bay Energy Corporation
Kébec Disc
McGill University
Ministère des Affaires culturelles
Ministère des Affaires intergouvernementales
Ministère des Affaires sociales
Ministère de l'Agriculture
Ministère des Communications
Ministère de l'Education
Ministère des Finances
Ministère de l'Industrie et du Commerce
Ministère des Richesses naturelles
Ministère des Terres et Forêts
Ministère du Tourisme, de la Chasse et de la Pêche
Ministère des Transports
Mirabel Airport
Monastère de l'Hôtel-Dieu de Québec
Montreal Canadiens
Montreal Expos
Montreal Museum of Fine Arts
Montreal Stock Exchange
Montreal Urban Community
Musée de l'Art Contemporain
Musée du Québec

National Film Board
National Hockey League
National Photography Collection
National Theatre School of Canada
Noranda Mines
Northern Quebec Inuit Association
Northern Telecom
Office National d'Oecumenisme
Alfred Pellan
Place des Arts, Montreal
Port of Montreal
Public Archives of Canada
Quebec Hospitals Association
Quebec Medical Association
Quebec Nordiques
Quebec Restaurant Association
Quebec Urban Community
Quebecair
Radio–Canada
Royal Victoria Hospital
Jean-Paul Ruleau
SOQUEM
The Seagram Company
Sidbec–Dosco
Société Historique du Saguenay
Transport Canada
Union Carbide Canada
Université de Laval
World Hockey Association

Canadian Cataloguing in Publication Data

Hocking, Anthony, 1944-
   Quebec

(Canada series)

Includes index.
ISBN 0-07-082691-9

1. Quebec (Province) . 2. Quebec (Province) — Description and travel.   I. Title.   II. Series.

FC2911.6.H63   971.4   C77-001600-6
F1052.5.H63

1 2 3 4 5 6 7 8 9 10   BP   7 6 5 4 3 2 1 0 9 8

Printed and bound in Canada

Index

CANADIAN STATISTICS

	Joined Confed- eration	Capital	Area	Population (1976)	Ethnic Origin (% 1971)		
					British	French	Other
CANADA		Ottawa	9 976 185 km²	22 992 604	45	29	26
Newfoundland	1949	St. John's	404 519 km²	557 725	94	3	3
Prince Edward Island	1873	Charlottetown	5 657 km²	118 229	83	14	3
Nova Scotia	1867	Halifax	55 491 km²	828 571	77	10	13
New Brunswick	1867	Fredericton	74 437 km²	677 250	58	37	5
Quebec	1867	Quebec City	1 540 687 km²	6 234 445	11	79	10
Ontario	1867	Toronto	1 068 587 km²	8 264 465	59	10	31
Manitoba	1870	Winnipeg	650 090 km²	1 021 506	42	9	49
Saskatchewan	1905	Regina	651 903 km²	921 323	42	6	52
Alberta	1905	Edmonton	661 188 km²	1 838 037	47	6	47
British Columbia	1871	Victoria	948 600 km²	2 466 608	58	4	38
Yukon	—	Whitehorse	536 327 km²	21 836	49	7	56
Northwest Territories	—	Yellowknife	3 379 699 km²	42 609	25	7	68